THE YALE CHRONICLES
OF AMERICA SERIES

The Fathers of the Constitution

A Chronicle of
the Establishment
of the Union

by
Max Farrand

1975

Toronto
Glasgow, Brook & Co.

New York
United States Publishers
Association, Inc.

Library of Congress Catalog Card No. 21-14805

International Standard Book No. 0-911548-12-2

CONTENTS

FATHERS OF THE CONSTITUTION

∴

CHAPTER I

THE TREATY OF PEACE

"The United States of America"! It was in the Declaration of Independence that this name was first and formally proclaimed to the world, and to maintain its verity the war of the Revolution was fought. Americans like to think that they were then assuming "among the Powers of the Earth the equal and independent Station to which the Laws of Nature and of Nature's God entitle them"; and, in view of their subsequent marvelous development, they are inclined to add that it must have been before an expectant world.

In these days of prosperity and national greatness it is hard to realize that the achievement of independence did not place the United States on a footing of equality with other countries and that, in fact, the new state was more or less an unwelcome member of the world family. It is nevertheless true that the latest comer into the family of nations did not for a long time command the respect of the world. This lack of respect was partly due to the character of the American population. Along with the many estimable and excellent people who had come to British North America inspired by the best of motives, there had come others who were not regarded favorably by the governing classes of Europe. Discontent is frequently a healthful sign and a forerunner of progress, but it makes one an uncomfortable neighbor in a satisfied and conservative community; and discontent was the underlying factor in the migration from the Old World to the New. In any composite immigrant population such as that of the United States there was bound to be a large element of undesirables. Among those who came "for conscience's sake" were the best type of religious protestants, but there were also religious cranks from many countries, of almost every conceivable sect and of no sect at all. Many of the newcomers were poor. It was common, too, to regard colonies as inferior places of residence to which objectionable persons might be encouraged to go and where the average of the population was lowered by the influx of convicts and thousands of slaves.

"The great number of emigrants from Europe" — wrote Thieriot, Saxon Commissioner of Commerce to America, from Philadelphia in 1784 — "has filled this place with worthless persons to such a degree that scarcely a day passes without theft, robbery, or even assassination."[1] It would perhaps be too much to say that the people of the United States were looked upon by the rest of the world as only half civilized, but certainly they were regarded as of lower social standing and of inferior quality, and many of them were known to be rough, uncultured, and ignorant. Great Britain and Germany maintained American missionary societies, not, as might perhaps be expected, for the benefit of the Indian or Negro, but for the poor, benighted colonists themselves; and Great Britain refused to commission a minister to her former colonies for nearly ten years after their independence had been recognized.

It is usually thought that the dregs of humiliation have been reached when the rights of foreigners are not considered safe in a particular country, so

[1] Quoted by W. E. Lingelbach, *History Teacher's Magazine*, March, 1913.

that another state insists upon establishing therein its own tribunal for the trial of its citizens or subjects. Yet that is what the French insisted upon in the United States, and they were supposed to be especially friendly. They had had their own experience in America. First the native Indian had appealed to their imagination. Then, at an appropriate moment, they seemed to see in the Americans a living embodiment of the philosophical theories of the time: they thought that they had at last found "the natural man" of Rousseau and Voltaire; they believed that they saw the social contract theory being worked out before their very eyes. Nevertheless, in spite of this interest in Americans, the French looked upon them as an inferior people over whom they would have liked to exercise a sort of protectorate. To them the Americans seemed to lack a proper knowledge of the amenities of life. Commissioner Thieriot, describing the administration of justice in the new republic, noticed that: "A Frenchman, with the prejudices of his country and accustomed to court sessions in which the officers have imposing robes and a uniform that makes it impossible to recognize them, smiles at seeing in the court room men dressed in street clothes, simple, often quite

common.   He is astonished to see the public enter
and leave the court room freely, those who prefer
even keeping their hats on."   Later he adds: "It
appears that the court of France wished to set up a
jurisdiction of its own on this continent for all matters involving French subjects."   France failed in
this; but at the very time that peace was under discussion Congress authorized Franklin to negotiate
a consular convention, ratified a few years later, according to which the citizens of the United States
and the subjects of the French King in the country
of the other should be tried by their respective consuls or vice-consuls.   Though this agreement was
made reciprocal in its terms and so saved appear-
ances for the honor of the new nation, nevertheless
in submitting it to Congress John Jay clearly
pointed out that it was reciprocal in name rather
than in substance, as there were few or no Americans in France but an increasing number of French-
men in the United States.

Such was the status of the new republic in the
family of nations when the time approached for the
negotiation of a treaty of peace with the mother
country.   The war really ended with the surrender of
Cornwallis at Yorktown in 1781.   Yet even then the
British were unwilling to concede the independence

of the revolted colonies.   This refusal of recognition was not merely a matter of pride; a division and a consequent weakening of the empire was involved; to avoid this Great Britain seems to have been willing to make any other concessions that were necessary.   The mother country sought to avoid disruption at all costs.   But the time had passed when any such adjustment might have been possible.   The Americans now flatly refused to treat of peace upon any footing except that of independent equality.   The British, being in no position to continue the struggle, were obliged to yield and to declare in the first article of the treaty of peace that "His Britannic Majesty acknowledges the said United States . . . to be free, sovereign, and independent states."

With France the relationship of the United States was clear and friendly enough at the time. The American War of Independence had been brought to a successful issue with the aid of France. In the treaty of alliance which had been signed in 1778 it had been agreed that neither France nor the United States should, without the consent of the other, make peace with Great Britain.   More than that, in 1781, partly out of gratitude but largely as a result of clever manipulation of factions in

Congress by the French Minister in Philadelphia, the Chevalier de la Luzerne, the American peace commissioners had been instructed "to make the most candid and confidential communications upon all subjects to the ministers of our generous ally, the King of France; to undertake nothing in the negotiations for peace or truce without their knowledge and concurrence; and ultimately to govern yourselves by their advice and opinion."[1] If France had been actuated only by unselfish motives in supporting the colonies in their revolt against Great Britain, these instructions might have been acceptable and even advisable. But such was not the case. France was working not so much with philanthropic purposes or for sentimental reasons as for the restoration to her former position of supremacy in Europe. Revenge upon England was only a part of a larger plan of national aggrandizement.

The treaty with France in 1778 had declared that war should be continued until the independence of the United States had been established, and it appeared as if that were the main purpose of the alliance. For her own good reasons France had dragged Spain into the struggle. Spain, of course, fought to cripple Great Britain and not to help the

[1] *Secret Journals of Congress*, June 15, 1781.

United States.   In return for this support **France**
was pledged to assist Spain in obtaining certain **ad-**
ditions to her territory.   In so far as these additions related to North America, the interests of
Spain and those of the United States were far from
being identical; in fact, they were frequently in direct opposition.   Spain was already in possession
of Louisiana and, by prompt action on her entry
into the war in 1780, she had succeeded in getting
control of eastern Louisiana and of practically all
the Floridas except St. Augustine.   To consolidate
these holdings and round out her American empire,
Spain would have liked to obtain the title to all the
land between the Alleghany Mountains and the
Mississippi.   Failing this, however, she seemed to
prefer that the region northwest of the Ohio River
should belong to the British rather than to the
United States.

Under these circumstances it was fortunate for
the United States that the American Peace Commissioners were broad-minded enough to appreciate
the situation and to act on their own responsibility.
Benjamin Franklin, although he was not the first to
be appointed, was generally considered to be the
chief of the Commission by reason of his age, experience, and reputation.   Over seventy-five years

old, he was more universally known and admired than probably any man of his time. This many-sided American — printer, almanac maker, writer, scientist, and philosopher — by the variety of his abilities as well as by the charm of his manner seemed to have found his real mission in the diplomatic field, where he could serve his country and at the same time, with credit to himself, preach his own doctrines.

When Franklin was sent to Europe at the outbreak of the Revolution, it was as if destiny had intended him for that particular task. His achievements had already attracted attention; in his fur cap and eccentric dress "he fulfilled admirably the Parisian ideal of the forest philosopher"; and with his facility in conversation, as well as by the attractiveness of his personality, he won both young and old. But, with his undoubted zeal for liberty and his unquestioned love of country, Franklin never departed from the Quaker principles he affected and always tried to avoid a fight. In these efforts, owing to his shrewdness and his willingness to compromise, he was generally successful.

John Adams, being then the American representative at The Hague, was the first Commissioner to be appointed. Indeed, when he was first named, in 1779, he was to be sole commissioner to negotiate peace; and it was the influential French Minister to the United States who was responsible for others being added to the commission. Adams was a sturdy New Englander of British stock and of a distinctly English type — medium height, a stout figure, and a ruddy face. No one questioned his honesty, his straightforwardness, or his lack of tact. Being a man of strong mind, of wide reading and even great learning, and having serene confidence in the purity of his motives as well as in the soundness of his judgment, Adams was little inclined to surrender his own views, and was ready to carry out his ideas against every obstacle. By nature as well as by training he seems to have been incapable of understanding the French; he was suspicious of them and he disapproved of Franklin's popularity even as he did of his personality.

Five Commissioners in all were named, but Thomas Jefferson and Henry Laurens did not take part in the negotiations, so that the only other active member was John Jay, then thirty-seven years old and already a man of prominence in his own country. Of French Huguenot stock and type, he was tall and slender, with somewhat of a scholar's stoop, and was usually dressed in black. His manners were gentle and unassuming, but his face, with its penetrating black eyes, its aquiline nose and pointed chin, revealed a proud and sensitive disposition. He had been sent to the court of Spain in 1780, and there he had learned enough to arouse his suspicions, if nothing more, of Spain's designs as well as of the French intention to support them.

In the spring of 1782 Adams felt obliged to remain at The Hague in order to complete the negotiations already successfully begun for a commercial treaty with the Netherlands. Franklin, thus the only Commissioner on the ground in Paris, began informal negotiations alone but sent an urgent call to Jay in Spain, who was convinced of the fruitlessness of his mission there and promptly responded. Jay's experience in Spain and his knowledge of Spanish hopes had led him to believe that the French were not especially concerned about American interests but were in fact willing to sacrifice them if necessary to placate Spain. He accordingly insisted that the American Commissioners should disregard their instructions and, without the knowledge of France, should deal directly with Great Britain. In this contention he was supported by Adams when he arrived, but it was hard to persuade Franklin to accept this point of view, for he was unwilling to believe anything so unworthy of his admiring and admired French. Nevertheless, with his cautious shrewdness, he finally yielded so far as to agree to see what might come out of direct negotiations.

The rest was relatively easy. Of course there were difficulties and such sharp differences of opinion that, even after long negotiation, some matters had to be compromised. Some problems, too, were found insoluble and were finally left without a settlement. But such difficulties as did exist were slight in comparison with the previous hopelessness of reconciling American and Spanish ambitions, especially when the latter were supported by France. On the one hand, the Americans were the protégés of the French and were expected to give way before the claims of their patron's friends to an extent which threatened to limit seriously their growth and development. On the other hand, they were the younger sons of England, uncivilized by their wilderness life, ungrateful and rebellious, but still to be treated by England as children of the blood. In the all-important question of extent of territory, where Spain and France would have limited the United States to the east of the Alleghany Mountains, Great Britain was persuaded

without great difficulty, having once conceded independence to the United States, to yield the
boundaries which she herself had formerly claimed
— from the Atlantic Ocean on the east to the
Mississippi River on the west, and from Canada on
the north to the southern boundary of Georgia.
Unfortunately the northern line, through ignorance
and carelessness rather than through malice, was
left uncertain at various points and became the
subject of almost continuous controversy until the
last bit of it was settled in 1911.[1]

The fisheries of the North Atlantic, for which
Newfoundland served as the chief focal point, had
been one of the great assets of North America from
the time of its discovery. They had been one of
the chief prizes at stake in the struggle between the
French and the British for the possession of the continent, and they had been of so much value that a
British statute of 1775 which cut off the New England fisheries was regarded, even after the "intoler-
able acts" of the previous year, as the height of
punishment for New England. Many Englishmen
would have been glad to see the Americans excluded from these fisheries, but John Adams, when

[1] See Lord Bryce's Introduction (p. xxiv) to W. A. Dunning,
The British Empire and the United States (1914).

he arrived from The Hague, displayed an appreciation of New England interests and the quality of his temper as well by flatly refusing to agree to any treaty which did not allow full fishing privileges. The British accordingly yielded and the Americans were granted fishing rights as "heretofore" enjoyed.   The right of navigation of the Mississippi River, it was declared in the treaty, should "forever remain free and open" to both parties; but here Great Britain was simply passing on to the United States a formal right which she had received from France and was retaining for herself a similar right which might sometime prove of use, for as long as Spain held both banks at the mouth of the Mississippi River, the right was of little practical value.

Two subjects involving the greatest difficulty of arrangement were the compensation of the Loyalists and the settlement of commercial indebtedness. The latter was really a question of the payment of British creditors by American debtors, for there was little on the other side of the balance sheet, and it seems as if the frugal Franklin would have preferred to make no concessions and would have allowed creditors to take their own chances of getting paid.   But the matter appeared to Adams in a different light — perhaps his New England conscience was aroused — and in this point of view he was supported by Jay. It was therefore finally agreed "that creditors on either side shall meet with no lawful impediment to the recovery of the full value in sterling money, of all *bona fide* debts heretofore contracted." However just this provision may have been, its incorporation in the terms of the treaty was a mistake on the part of the Commissioners, because the Government of the United States had no power to give effect to such an arrangement, so that the provision had no more value than an emphatic expression of opinion. Accordingly, when some of the States later disregarded this part of the treaty, the British had an excuse for refusing to carry out certain of their own obligations.

The historian of the Virginia Federal Convention of 1788, H. B. Grigsby, relates an amusing incident growing out of the controversy over the payment of debts to creditors in England:

A Scotchman, John Warden, a prominent lawyer and good classical scholar, but suspected rightly of Tory leanings during the Revolution, learning of the large minority against the repeal of laws in conflict with the treaty of 1783 (*i. e.*, especially the laws as to the collection of debts by foreigners) caustically remarked that some of the members of the House had voted against paying for the coats on their backs. The story goes that he was summoned before the House in full session, and was compelled to beg their pardon on his knees; but as he rose, pretending to brush the dust from his knees, he pointed to the House and said audibly, with evident double meaning, "Upon my word, a dommed dirty house it is indeed." The Journal of the House, however, shows that the honor of the delegates was satisfied by a written assurance from Mr. Warden that he meant in no way to affront the dignity of the House or to insult any of its members.

The other question, that of compensating the Loyalists for the loss of their property, was not so simple a matter, for the whole story of the Revolution was involved. There is a tendency among many scholars of the present day to regard the policy of the British toward their North American colonies as possibly unwise and blundering but as being entirely in accordance with the legal and constitutional rights of the mother country, and to believe that the Americans, while they may have been practically and therefore morally justified in asserting their independence, were still technically and legally in the wrong. It is immaterial whether or not that point of view is accepted, for its mere recognition is sufficient to explain the existence of a large number of Americans who were steadfast in their support of the British side of the controversy. Indeed, it has been estimated that as large a proportion as one-third of the population remained loyal to the Crown. Numbers must remain more or less uncertain, but probably the majority of the people in the United States, whatever their feelings may have been, tried to remain neutral or at least to appear so; and it is undoubtedly true that the Revolution was accomplished by an aggressive minority and that perhaps as great a number were actively loyal to Great Britain.

These Loyalists comprised at least two groups. One of these was a wealthy, property-owning class, representing the best social element in the colonies, extremely conservative, believing in privilege and fearing the rise of democracy. The other was composed of the royal office-holders, which included some of the better families, but was more largely made up of the lower class of political and social hangers-on, who had been rewarded with these positions for political debts incurred in England. The opposition of both groups to the Revolution was inevitable and easily to be understood, but it was also natural that the Revolutionists should incline to hold the Loyalists, without distinction, largely responsible for British pre-Revolutionary policy, asserting that they misinformed the Government as to conditions and sentiment in America, partly through stupidity and partly through selfish interest.   It was therefore perfectly comprehensible that the feeling should be bitter against them in the United States, especially as they had given efficient aid to the British during the war.   In various States they were subjected to personal violence at the hands of indignant "patriots," many being forced to flee from their homes, while their property was destroyed or confiscated, and frequently these acts were legalized by statute.

The historian of the Loyalists of Massachusetts, James H. Stark, must not be expected to understate the case, but when he is describing, especially in New England, the reign of terror which was established to suppress these people, he writes:

Loyalists were tarred and feathered and carried on rails, gagged and bound for days at a time; stoned, fastened in a room with a fire and the chimney stopped on top; advertised as public enemies, so that they would be cut off from all dealings with their neighbors; they had bullets shot into their bedrooms, their horses poisoned or mutilated; money or valuable plate extorted from them to save them from violence, and on pretence of taking security for their good behavior; their houses and ships burned; they were compelled to pay the guards who watched them in their houses, and when carted about for the mob to stare at and abuse, they were compelled to pay something at every town.

There is little doubt also that the confiscation of property and the expulsion of the owners from the community were helped on by people who were debtors to the Loyalists and in this way saw a chance of escaping from the payment of their rightful obligations. The " Act for confiscating the estates of certain persons commonly called absentees " may have been a measure of self-defense for the State but it was passed by the votes of those who undoubtedly profited by its provisions.

Those who had stood loyally by the Crown must in turn be looked out for by the British Government, especially when the claims of justice were reinforced by the important consideration that many of those with property and financial interests in America were relatives of influential persons in England. The immediate necessity during the war had been partially met by assisting thousands to go to Canada — where their descendants today form an important element in the population and are proud of being United Empire Loyalists — while pensions and gifts were supplied to others. Now that the war was over the British were determined that Americans should make good to the

Loyalists for all that they had suffered, and His Majesty's Commissioners were hopeful at least of obtaining a proviso similar to the one relating to the collection of debts. John Adams, however, expressed the prevailing American idea when he said that "paying debts and compensating Tories" were two very different things, and Jay asserted that there were certain of these refugees whom Americans never would forgive.

But this was the one thing needed to complete the negotiations for peace, and the British arguments on the injustice and irregularity of the treatment accorded to the Loyalists were so strong that the American Commissioners were finally driven to the excuse that the Government of the Confederation had no power over the individual States by whom the necessary action must be taken. Finally, in a spirit of mutual concession at the end of the negotiations, the Americans agreed that Congress should "recommend to the legislatures of the respective states to provide for the restitution" of properties which had been confiscated "belonging to real British subjects," and "that persons of any other description" might return to the United States for a period of twelve months and be "unmolested in their endeavours to obtain the restitution."

With this show of yielding on the part of the American Commissioners it was possible to conclude the terms of peace, and the preliminary treaty was drawn accordingly and agreed to on November 30, 1782. Franklin had been of such great service during all the negotiations, smoothing down ruffled feelings by his suavity and tact and presenting difficult subjects in a way that made action possible, that to him was accorded the unpleasant task of communicating what had been accomplished to Vergennes, the French Minister, and of requesting at the same time "a fresh loan of twenty million francs." Franklin, of course, presented his case with much "delicacy and kindliness of manner" and with a fair degree of success. "Vergennes thought that the signing of the articles was premature, but he made no inconvenient remonstrances, and procured six millions of the twenty."[1] On September 3, 1783, the definite treaty of peace was signed and in due time it was ratified by the British Parliament as well as by the American Congress. The new state, duly accredited, thus took its place in the family of nations; but it was a very humble place that was first assigned to the United States of America.

[1] Channing, *History of the United States*, vol. iii, p. 368.

CHAPTER II

THOUGH the word revolution implies a violent break with the past, there was nothing in the Revolution that transformed the essential character or the characteristics of the American people. The Revolution severed the ties which bound the colonies to Great Britain; it created some new activities; some soldiers were diverted from their former trades and occupation; but, as the proportion of the population engaged in the war was relatively small and the area of country affected for any length of time was comparatively slight, it is safe to say that in general the mass of the people remained about the same after the war as before. The professional man was found in his same calling; the artisan returned to his tools, if he had ever laid them down; the shopkeeper resumed his business, if it had been interrupted; the merchant went back to his trading; and the farmer before the Revolution remained a farmer afterward.

The country as a whole was in relatively good condition and the people were reasonably prosperous; at least, there was no general distress or poverty. Suffering had existed in the regions ravaged by war, but no section had suffered unduly or had had to bear the burden of war during the entire period of fighting. American products had been in demand, especially in the West India Islands, and an illicit trade with the enemy had sprung up, so that even during the war shippers were able to dispose of their commodites at good prices. The Americans are commonly said to have been an agricultural people, but it would be more correct to say that the great majority of the people were dependent upon extractive industries, which would include lumbering, fishing, and even the fur trade, as well as the ordinary agricultural pursuits. Save for a few industries, of which shipbuilding was one of the most important, there was relatively little manufacturing apart from the household crafts. These household industries had increased during the war, but as it was with the individual so it was with the whole country; the general course of industrial activity was much the same as it had been before the war.

A fundamental fact is to be observed in the

economy of the young nation: the people were raising far more tobacco and grain and were extracting
far more of other products than they could possibly
use themselves; for the surplus they must find markets.   They had, as well, to rely upon the outside
world for a great part of their manufactured goods,
especially for those of the higher grade.   In other
words, from the economic point of view, the United
States remained in the former colonial stage of industrial dependence, which was aggravated rather
than alleviated by the separation from Great Britain.   During the colonial period, Americans had
carried on a large amount of this external trade by
means of their own vessels.   The British Navigation Acts required the transportation of goods in
British vessels, manned by crews of British sailors,
and specified certain commodities which could be
shipped to Great Britain only.   They also required
that much of the European trade should pass by
way of England.   But colonial vessels and colonial
sailors came under the designation of "British,"
and no small part of the prosperity of New England,
and of the middle colonies as well, had been due to
the carrying trade.   It would seem therefore as if a
primary need of the American people immediately
after the Revolution was to get access to their old

markets and to carry the goods as much as possible in their own vessels.

In some directions they were successful. One of the products in greatest demand was fish. The fishing industry had been almost annihilated by the war, but with the establishment of peace the New England fisheries began to recover. They were in competition with the fishermen of France and England who were aided by large bounties, yet the superior geographical advantages which the American fishermen possessed enabled them to maintain and expand their business, and the rehabilitation of the fishing fleet was an important feature of their programme. In other directions they were not so successful. The British still believed in their colonial system and applied its principles without regard to the interests of the United States. Such American products as they wanted they allowed to be carried to British markets, but in British vessels. Certain commodities, the production of which they wished to encourage within their own dominions, they added to the prohibited list. Americans cried out indignantly that this was an attempt on the part of the British to punish their former colonies for their temerity in revolting. The British Government may well have derived some satisfaction from the fact that certain restrictions bore heavily upon New England, as John Adams complained; but it would seem to be much nearer the truth to say that in a truly characteristic way the British were phlegmatically attending to their own interests and calmly ignoring the United States, and that there was little malice in their policy.

European nations had regarded American trade as a profitable field of enterprise and as probably responsible for much of Great Britain's prosperity. It was therefore a relatively easy matter for the United States to enter into commercial treaties with foreign countries. These treaties, however, were not fruitful of any great result; for, "with unimportant exceptions, they left still in force the high import duties and prohibitions that marked the European tariffs of the time, as well as many features of the old colonial system. They were designed to legalize commerce rather than to encourage it."[1] Still, for a year or more after the war the demand for American products was great enough to satisfy almost everybody. But in 1784 France and Spain closed their colonial ports and thus excluded the shipping of the United States. This

[1] Clive Day, *Encyclopedia of American Government,* vol. i, p. 340.

proved to be so disastrous for their colonies that the French Government soon was forced to relax its restrictions. The British also made some concessions, and where their orders were not modified they were evaded. And so, in the course of a few years, the West India trade recovered.

More astonishing to the men of that time than it is to us was the fact that American foreign trade fell under British commercial control again. Whether it was that British merchants were accustomed to American ways of doing things and knew American business conditions; whether other countries found the commerce not as profitable as they had expected, as certainly was the case with France; whether "American merchants and sea captains found themselves under disadvantages due to the absence of treaty protection which they had enjoyed as English subjects";[1] or whether it was the necessity of trading on British capital — whatever the cause may have been — within a comparatively few years a large part of American trade was in British hands as it had been before the Revolution. American trade with Europe was carried on through English merchants very much as the Navigation Acts had prescribed.

[1] C. R. Fish, *American Diplomacy*, pp. 56–57.

From the very first settlement of the American continent the colonists had exhibited one of the earliest and most lasting characteristics of the American people — adaptability. The Americans now proceeded to manifest that trait anew, not only by adjusting themselves to renewed commercial dependence upon Great Britain, but by seeking new avenues of trade. A striking illustration of this is to be found in the development of trade with the Far East. Captain Cook's voyage around the world (1768–1771), an account of which was first published in London in 1773, attracted a great deal of attention in America; an edition of the *New Voyage* was issued in New York in 1774. No sooner was the Revolution over than there began that romantic trade with China and the northwest coast of America, which made the fortunes of some families of Salem and Boston and Philadelphia. This commerce added to the prosperity of the country, but above all it stimulated the imagination of Americans. In the same way another outlet was found in trade with Russia by way of the Baltic.

The foreign trade of the United States after the Revolution thus passed through certain well-marked phases. First there was a short period of prosperity, owing to an unusual demand for American products; this was followed by a longer period of depression; and then came a gradual recovery through acceptance of the new conditions and adjustment to them.

A similar cycle may be traced in the domestic or internal trade. In early days intercolonial commerce had been carried on mostly by water, and when war interfered commerce almost ceased for want of roads. The loss of ocean highways, however, stimulated road building and led to what might be regarded as the first "good-roads movement" of the new nation, except that to our eyes it would be a misuse of the word to call any of those roads good. But anything which would improve the means of transportation took on a patriotic tinge, and the building of roads and the cutting of canals were agitated until turnpike and canal companies became a favorite form of investment; and in a few years the interstate land trade had grown to considerable importance. But in the meantime, water transportation was the main reliance, and with the end of the war the coastwise trade had been promptly resumed. For a time it prospered; but the States, affected by the general economic conditions and by jealousy, tried to interfere with and divert the trade of others to their own advantage. This was done by imposing fees and charges and duties, not merely upon goods and vessels from abroad but upon those of their fellow States. James Madison described the situation in the words so often quoted: "Some of the States, . . . having no convenient ports for foreign commerce, were subject to be taxed by their neighbors, thro whose ports, their commerce was carryed on. New Jersey, placed between Phila. & N. York, was likened to a Cask tapped at both ends: and N. Carolina between Virga. & S. Carolina to a patient bleeding at both Arms."[1]

The business depression which very naturally followed the short revival of trade was so serious in its financial consequences that it has even been referred to as the "Panic of 1785." The United States afforded a good market for imported articles in 1783 and 1784, all the better because of the supply of gold and silver which had been sent into the country by England and France to maintain their armies and fleets and which had remained in the United States. But this influx of imported goods was one of the chief factors in causing the depression of 1785, as it brought ruin to many of

[1] *Records of the Federal Convention*, vol. iii, p. 542.

those domestic industries which had sprung up in the days of non-intercourse or which had been stimulated by the artificial protection of the war.

To make matters worse, the currency was in a confused condition. "In 1784 the entire coin of the land, except coppers, was the product of foreign mints.   English guineas, crowns, shillings and pence were still paid over the counters of shops and taverns, and with them were mingled many French and Spanish and some German coins. . . .   The value of the gold pieces expressed in dollars was pretty much the same the country over.   But the dollar and the silver pieces regarded as fractions of a dollar had no less than five different values."[1] The importation of foreign goods was fast draining the hard money out of the country.   In an effort to relieve the situation but with the result of making it much worse, several of the States began to issue paper money; and this was in addition to the enormous quantities of paper which had been printed during the Revolution and which was now worth but a small fraction of its face value.

The expanding currency and consequent depreciation in the value of money had immediately

[1] McMaster, *History of the People of the United States*, vol. i, pp. 190–191.

resulted in a corresponding rise of prices, which for a while the States attempted to control.   But in 1778 Congress threw up its hands in despair and voted that "all limitations of prices of gold and silver be taken off," although the States for some time longer continued to endeavor to regulate prices by legislation.[1]   The fluctuating value of the currency increased the opportunities for speculation which war conditions invariably offer, and "immense fortunes were suddenly accumulated." A new financial group rose into prominence composed largely of those who were not accustomed to the use of money and who were consequently inclined to spend it recklessly and extravagantly.

Many contemporaries comment upon these things, of whom Brissot de Warville may be taken as an example, although he did not visit the United States until 1788:

The inhabitants . . . prefer the splendor of wealth and the show of enjoyment to the simplicity of manners and the pure pleasures which result from it.   If there is a town on the American continent where the English luxury displays its follies, it is New York. You will find here the English fashions: in the dress of the women you will see the most brilliant silks, gauzes,

[1] W. E. H. Lecky, *The American Revolution*, New York, 1898, pp. 288–294.

hats, and borrowed hair; equipages are rare, but they are elegant; the men have more simplicity in their dress; they disdain gewgaws, but they take their revenge in the luxury of the table; luxury forms already a class of men very dangerous to society; I mean bachelors; the expense of women causes matrimony to be dreaded by men. Tea forms, as in England, the basis of parties of pleasure; many things are dearer here than in France; a hairdresser asks twenty shilling a month; washing costs four shillings a dozen.[1]

An American writer of a later date, looking back upon his earlier years, was impressed by this same extravagance, and his testimony may well be used to strengthen the impression which it is the purpose of the present narrative to convey:

The French and British armies circulated immense sums of money in gold and silver coin, which had the effect of driving out of circulation the wretched paper currency which had till then prevailed. Immense quantities of British and French goods were soon imported: our people imbibed a taste for foreign fashions and luxury; and in the course of two or three years, from the close of the war, such an entire change had taken place in the habits and manners of our inhabitants, that it almost appeared as if we had suddenly become a different nation. The staid and sober habits of our ancestors, with their plain home-manufactured clothing,

[1] Quoted by Henry Tuckerman, *America and her Commentators*, 1864.

were suddenly laid aside, and European goods of fine quality adopted in their stead.   Fine ruffles, powdered heads, silks and scarlets, decorated the men; while the most costly silks, satins, chintzes, calicoes, muslins, etc., etc., decorated our females.   Nor was their diet less expensive; for superb plate, foreign spirits, wines, etc., etc., sparkled on the sideboards of many farmers. The natural result of this change of the habits and customs of the people — this aping of European manners and morals, — was to suddenly drain our country of its circulating specie; and as a necessary consequence, the people ran in debt, times became difficult, and money hard to raise.[1]

The situation was serious, and yet it was not as dangerous or even as critical as it has generally been represented, because the fundamental bases of American prosperity were untouched.   The way by which Americans could meet the emergency and recover from the hard times was fairly evident — first to economize, and then to find new outlets for their industrial energies.   But the process of adjustment was slow and painful.   There were not a few persons in the United States who were even disposed to regret that Americans were not safely under British protection and prospering with Great Britain, instead of suffering in political isolation.

[1] Samuel Kercheval, *History of the Valley of Virginia*, 1833, pp. 199–200.

CHAPTER III

WHEN peace came in 1783 there were in the United States approximately three million people, who were spread over the whole Atlantic coast from Maine to Georgia and back into the interior as far as the Alleghany Mountains; and a relatively small number of settlers had crossed the mountain barrier. About twenty per cent of the population, or some six hundred thousand, were Negro slaves. There was also a large alien element of foreign birth or descent, poor when they arrived in America, and, although they had been able to raise themselves to a position of comparative comfort, life among them was still crude and rough. Many of the people were poorly educated and lacking in cultivation and refinement and in a knowledge of the usages of good society. Not only were they looked down upon by other nations of the world; there was within the United States itself a relatively small upper class inclined to regard the mass of the people as of an inferior order.

Thus, while forces were at work favorable to democracy, the gentry remained in control of affairs after the Revolution, although their numbers were reduced by the emigration of the Loyalists and their power was lessened.   The explanation of this aristocratic control may be found in the fact that the generation of the Revolution had been accustomed to monarchy and to an upper class and that the people were wont to take their ideas and to accept suggestions from their betters without question or murmur.   This deferential attitude is attested by the indifference of citizens to the right of voting.   By about 1919, before the great extension of woman suffrage, the number of persons voting approximated twenty per cent of the population, but after the Revolution less than five per cent of the white population voted.   There were many limitations upon the exercise of the suffrage, but the small number of voters was only partially due to these restrictions, for in later years, without any radical change in suffrage qualifications, the proportion of citizens who voted steadily increased.

The fact is that many of the people did not care to vote.   Why should they, when they were only registering the will or the wishes of their superiors? But among the relatively small number who constituted the governing class there was a high standard of intelligence. Popular magazines were unheard of and newspapers were infrequent, so that men depended largely upon correspondence and personal intercourse for the interchange of ideas. There was time, however, for careful reading of the few available books; there was time for thought, for writing, for discussion, and for social intercourse. It hardly seems too much to say, therefore, that there was seldom, if ever, a people — certainly never a people scattered over so wide a territory — who knew so much about government as did this controlling element of the people of the United States.

The practical character, as well as the political genius, of the Americans was never shown to better advantage than at the outbreak of the Revolution, when the quarrel with the mother country was manifesting itself in the conflict between the Governors, and other appointed agents of the Crown, and the popularly elected houses of the colonial legislatures. When the Crown resorted to dissolving the legislatures, the revolting colonists kept up and observed the forms of government. When the legislature was prevented from meeting, the members

would come together and call themselves a congress
or a convention, and, instead of adopting laws or
orders, would issue what were really nothing more
than recommendations, but which they expected
would be obeyed by their supporters. To enforce
these recommendations extra-legal committees,
generally backed by public opinion and sometimes
concretely supported by an organized "mob,"
would meet in towns and counties and would be
often effectively centralized where the opponents
of the British policy were in control.

In several of the colonies the want of orderly
government became so serious that, in 1775, the
Continental Congress advised them to form temporary governments until the trouble with Great
Britain had been settled. When independence
was declared Congress recommended to all the
States that they should adopt governments of their
own. In accordance with that recommendation,
in the course of a very few years each State established an independent government and adopted a
written constitution. It was a time when men believed in the social contract or the "compact theory
of the state," that states originated through agreement, as the case might be, between king and nobles, between king and people, or among the people

themselves.   In support of this doctrine no less an authority than the Bible was often quoted, such a passage for example as II Samuel v, 3: "So all the elders of Israel came to the King to Hebron; and King David made a covenant with them in Hebron before the Lord; and they anointed David King over Israel."   As a philosophical speculation to explain why people were governed or consented to be governed, this theory went back at least to the Greeks, and doubtless much earlier; and, though of some significance in medieval thought, it became of greater importance in British political philosophy, especially through the works of Thomas Hobbes and John Locke.   A very practical application of the compact theory was made in the English Revolution of 1688, when in order to avoid the embarrassment of deposing the king, the convention of the Parliament adopted the resolution: "That King James the Second, having endeavored to subvert the Constitution of the Kingdom, by breaking the original Contract between King and People, and having, by the advice of Jesuits, and other wicked persons, violated the fundamental Laws, and withdrawn himself out of this Kingdom, has abdicated the Government, and that the throne is hereby vacant."   These theories were developed by Jean

Jacques Rousseau in his *Contrat Social* — a book so attractively written that it eclipsed all other works upon the subject and resulted in his being regarded as the author of the doctrine — and through him they spread all over Europe.

Conditions in America did more than lend color to pale speculation; they seemed to take this hypothesis out of the realm of theory and to give it practical application.   What happened when men went into the wilderness to live?   The Pilgrim Fathers on board the *Mayflower* entered into an agreement which was signed by the heads of families who took part in the enterprise: "We, whose names are underwritten . . . Do by these presents, solemnly and mutually, in the Presence of God and one another, covenant and combine ourselves together into a civil Body Politick."

Other colonies, especially in New England, with this example before them of a social contract entered into similar compacts or "plantation covenants," as they were called.   But the colonists were also accustomed to having written charters granted which continued for a time at least to mark the extent of governmental powers.   Through this intermingling of theory and practice it was the most

natural thing in the world, when Americans came
to form their new State Governments, that they
should provide written instruments framed by their
own representatives, which not only bound them
to be governed in this way but also placed limitations upon the governing bodies. As the first
great series of written constitutions, these frames
of government attracted wide attention. Congress printed a set for general distribution, and
numerous editions were circulated both at home
and abroad.

The constitutions were brief documents, varying
from one thousand to twelve thousand words in
length, which established the framework of the
governmental machinery. Most of them, before
proceeding to practical working details, enunciated
a series of general principles upon the subject of
government and political morality in what were
called declarations or bills of rights. The character of these declarations may be gathered from the
following excerpts:

That all men are by nature equally free and independent, and have certain inherent rights, . . . the
enjoyment of life and liberty, with the means of acquiring and possessing property, and pursuing and
obtaining happiness and safety.

That no man, or set of men, are entitled to exclusive or separate emoluments or privileges from the community, but in consideration of public services.

The body politic is formed by a voluntary association of individuals; it is a social compact by which the whole people covenants with each citizen and each citizen with the whole people that all shall be governed by certain laws for the common good.

That all power of suspending laws, or the execution of laws, by any authority, without consent of the representatives of the people, is injurious to their rights, and ought not to be exercised.

That general warrants, . . . are grievous and oppressive, and ought not to be granted.

All penalties ought to be proportioned to the nature of the offence.

That sanguinary laws ought to be avoided, as far as is consistent with the safety of the State; and no law, to inflict cruel and unusual pains and penalties, ought to be made in any case, or at any time hereafter.

No magistrate or court of law shall demand excessive bail or sureties, impose excessive fines . . .

Every individual has a natural and unalienable right to worship God according to the dictates of his own conscience, and reason; . . .

That the freedom of the press is one of the great bulwarks of liberty, and can never be restrained but by despotic governments.

It will be perceived at once that these are but variations of the English Declaration of Rights of 1689, which indeed was consciously followed as a model; and yet there is a world-wide difference between the English model and these American copies. The earlier document enunciated the rights of English subjects, the recent infringement of which made it desirable that they should be reasserted in convincing form. The American documents asserted rights which the colonists generally had enjoyed and which they declared to be "governing principles for all peoples in all future times."

But the greater significance of these State Constitutions is to be found in their quality as working instruments of government. There was indeed little difference between the old colonial and the new State Governments. The inhabitants of each of the Thirteen States had been accustomed to a large measure of self-government, and when they took matters into their own hands they were not disposed to make any radical changes in the forms to which they had become accustomed. Accordingly the State Governments that were adopted simply continued a framework of government almost identical with that of colonial times.   To be sure, the Governor and other appointed officials were now elected either by the people or the legislature, and so were ultimately responsible to the electors instead of to the Crown; and other changes were made which in the long run might prove of far-reaching and even of vital significance; and yet the machinery of government seemed the same as that to which the people were already accustomed. The average man was conscious of no difference at all in the working of the Government under the new order.   In fact, in Connecticut and Rhode Island, the most democratic of all the colonies, where the people had been privileged to elect their own governors, as well as legislatures, no change whatever was necessary and the old charters were continued as State Constitutions down to 1818 and 1842, respectively.

To one who has been accustomed to believe that the separation from a monarchical government meant the establishment of democracy, a reading of these first State Constitutions is likely to cause a rude shock.   A shrewd English observer, traveling a generation later in the United States, went to the root of the whole matter in remarking of the Americans that, "When their independence was achieved their mental condition was not instantly changed. Their deference for rank and for judicial and legislative authority continued nearly unimpaired."[1] They might declare that "all men are created equal," and bills of rights might assert that government rested upon the consent of the governed; but these constitutions carefully provided that such consent should come from property owners, and, in many of the States, from religious believers and even followers of the Christian faith. "The man of small means might vote, but none save well-to-do Christians could legislate, and in many states none but a rich Christian could be a governor."[2] In South Carolina, for example, a freehold of £10,000 currency was required of the Governor, Lieutenant Governor, and members of the Council; £2,000 of the members of the Senate; and, while every elector was eligible to the House of Representatives, he had to acknowledge the being of a God and to believe in a future state of rewards and punishments, as well as to hold "a freehold at least of fifty acres of land, or a town lot."

[1] George Combe, *Tour of the United States*, vol. i, p. 205.
[2] McMaster, *Acquisition of Industrial, Popular, and Political Rights of Man in America*, p. 20.

It was government by a property-owning class, but in comparison with other countries this class represented a fairly large and increasing proportion of the population. In America the opportunity of becoming a property-owner was open to every one, or, as that phrase would then have been understood, to most white men. This system of class control is illustrated by the fact that, with the exception of Massachusetts, the new State Constitutions were never submitted to the people for approval.

The democratic sympathizer of today is inclined to point to those first State Governments as a continuance of the old order. But to the conservative of that time it seemed as if radical and revolutionary changes were taking place. The bills of rights declared, "That no men, or set of men, are entitled to exclusive or separate emoluments or privileges from the community, but in consideration of public services." Property qualifications and other restrictions on office-holding and the exercise of the suffrage were lessened. Four States declared in their constitutions against the entailment of estates, and primogeniture was abolished in aristocratic Virginia. There was a fairly complete abolition of all vestiges of feudal tenure in the holding of land, so that it may be said that in this period full ownership of property was established. The further separation of church and state was also carried out.

Certainly leveling influences were at work, and the people as a whole had moved one step farther in the direction of equality and democracy, and it was well that the Revolution was not any more radical and revolutionary than it was. The change was gradual and therefore more lasting. One finds readily enough contemporary statements to the effect that, "Although there are no nobles in America, there is a class of men denominated 'gentlemen,' who, by reason of their wealth, their talents, their education, their families, or the offices they hold, aspire to a preëminence," but, the same observer adds, this is something which "the people refuse to grant them." Another contemporary contributes the observation that there was not so much respect paid to gentlemen of rank as there should be, and that the lower orders of people behave as if they were on a footing of equality with them.

Whether the State Constitutions are to be regarded as property protection, aristocratic instruments, or as progressive documents, depends upon the point of view. And so it is with the spirit of union or of nationality in the United States. One student emphasizes the fact of there being "thirteen independent republics differing . . . widely in climate, in soil, in occupation, in everything which makes up the social and economic life of the people"; while another sees "the United States a nation." There is something to be said for both sides, and doubtless the truth lies between them, for there were forces making for disintegration as well as for unification. To the student of the present day, however, the latter seem to have been the stronger and more important, although the possibility was never absent that the thirteen States would go their separate ways.

There are few things so potent as a common danger to bring discordant elements into working harmony. Several times in the century and a half of their existence, when the colonies found themselves threatened by their enemies, they had united, or at least made an effort to unite, for mutual help. The New England Confederation of 1643 was organized primarily for protection against the Indians and incidentally against the Dutch and French. Whenever trouble threatened with any of the European powers or with the Indians — and that was frequently — a plan would be broached for getting the colonies to combine their efforts, sometimes for the immediate necessity and sometimes for a broader purpose.   The best known of these plans was that presented to the Albany Congress of 1754, which had been called to make effective preparation for the inevitable struggle with the French and Indians.   The beginning of the troubles which culminated in the final breach with Great Britain had quickly brought united action in the form of the Stamp Act Congress of 1765, in the Committees of Correspondence, and then in the Continental Congress.

It was not merely that the leaven of the Revolution was already working to bring about the freer interchange of ideas; instinct and experience led the colonies to united action.   The very day that the Continental Congress appointed a committee to frame a declaration of independence, another committee was ordered to prepare articles of union. A month later, as soon as the Declaration of Independence had been adopted, this second committee, of which John Dickinson of Pennsylvania was chairman, presented to Congress a report in the form of Articles of Confederation.   Although the outbreak of fighting made some sort of united action imperative, this plan of union was subjected to debate intermittently for over sixteen months and even after being adopted by Congress, toward the end of 1777, it was not ratified by the States until March, 1781, when the war was already drawing to a close.   The exigencies of the hour forced Congress, without any authorization, to act as if it had been duly empowered and in general to proceed as if the Confederation had been formed.

Benjamin Franklin was an enthusiast for union. It was he who had submitted the plan of union to the Albany Congress in 1754, which with modifications was recommended by that congress for adoption.   It provided for a Grand Council of representatives chosen by the legislature of each colony, the members to be proportioned to the contribution of that colony to the American military service.   In matters concerning the colonies as a whole, especially in Indian affairs, the Grand Council was to be given extensive powers of legislation and taxation. The executive was to be a President or Governor-General, appointed and paid by the Crown, with the right of nominating all military officers, and with a veto upon all acts of the Grand Council. The project was far in advance of the times and ultimately failed of acceptance, but in 1775, with the beginning of the troubles with Great Britain, Franklin took his Albany plan and, after modifying it in accordance with the experience of twenty years, submitted it to the Continental Congress as a new plan of government under which the colonies might unite.

Franklin's plan of 1775 seems to have attracted little attention in America, and possibly it was not generally known; but much was made of it abroad, where it soon became public, probably in the same way that other Franklin papers came out. It seems to have been his practice to make, with his own hand, several copies of such a document, which he would send to his friends with the statement that as the document in question was confidential they might not otherwise see a copy of it. Of course the inevitable happened, and such documents found their way into print to the apparent surprise and dismay of the author. Incidentally this practice caused confusion in later years, because each possessor of such a document would claim that he had the original. Whatever may have been the procedure in this particular case, it is fairly evident that Dickinson's committee took Franklin's plan of 1775 as the starting point of its work, and after revision submitted it to Congress as their report; for some of the most important features of the Articles of Confederation are to be found, sometimes word for word, in Franklin's draft.

This explanation of the origin of the Articles of Confederation is helpful and perhaps essential in understanding the form of government established, because that government in its main features had been devised for an entirely different condition of affairs, when a strong, centralized government would not have been accepted even if it had been wanted.   It provided for a "league of friendship," with the primary purpose of considering preparation for action rather than of taking the initiative. Furthermore, the final stages of drafting the Articles of Confederation had occurred at the outbreak of the war, when the people of the various States were showing a disposition to follow readily suggestions that came from those whom they could trust and when they seemed to be willing to submit without compulsion to orders from the same source.   These circumstances, quite as much as the inexperience of Congress and the jealousy of the States, account for the inefficient form of government which was devised; and inefficient the Confederation certainly was.   The only organ of government was a Congress in which every State was entitled to one vote and was represented by a delegation whose members were appointed annually as the legislature of the State might direct, whose expenses were paid by the State, and who were subject to recall. In other words, it was a council of States whose representatives had little incentive to independence of action.

Extensive powers were granted to this Congress "of determining on peace and war, . . . of entering into treaties and alliances," of maintaining an army and a navy, of establishing post offices, of coining money, and of making requisitions upon the States for their respective share of expenses "incurred for the common defence or general welfare." But none of these powers could be exercised without the consent of nine States, which was equivalent to requiring a two-thirds vote, and even when such a vote had been obtained and a decision had been reached, there was nothing to compel the individual States to obey beyond the mere declaration in the Articles of Confederation that, "Every State shall abide by the determinations of the United States in Congress assembled."

No executive was provided for except that Congress was authorized "to appoint such other committees and civil officers as may be necessary for managing the general affairs of the United States.

under their direction." In judicial matters, Congress was to serve as "the last resort on appeal in all disputes and differences" between States; and Congress might establish courts for the trial of piracy and felonies committed on the high seas and for determining appeals in cases of prize capture.

The plan of a government was there but it lacked any driving force. Congress might declare war but the States might decline to participate in it; Congress might enter into treaties but it could not make the States live up to them; Congress might borrow money but it could not be sure of repaying it; and Congress might decide disputes without being able to make the parties accept the decision. The pressure of necessity might keep the States together for a time, yet there is no disguising the fact that the Articles of Confederation formed nothing more than a gentlemen's agreement.

CHAPTER IV

THE population of the United States was like a body of water that was being steadily enlarged by internal springs and external tributaries. It was augmented both from within and from without, from natural increase and from immigration. It had spread over the whole coast from Maine to Georgia and slowly back into the interior, at first along the lines of river communication and then gradually filling up the spaces between until the larger part of the available land east of the Alleghany Mountains was settled. There the stream was checked as if dammed by the mountain barrier, but the population was trickling through wherever it could find an opening, slowly wearing channels, until finally, when the obstacles were overcome, it broke through with a rush.

Twenty years before the Revolution the expanding population had reached the mountains and was

ready to go beyond.   The difficulty of crossing the
mountains was not insuperable, but the French and
Indian War, followed by Pontiac's Conspiracy,
made outlying frontier settlement dangerous if not
impossible.   The arbitrary restriction of western
settlement by the Proclamation of 1763 did not
stop the more adventurous but did hold back the
mass of the population until near the time of the
Revolution, when a few bands of settlers moved
into Kentucky and Tennessee and rendered important but inconspicuous service in the fighting.
But so long as the title to that territory was in
doubt no considerable body of people would move
into it, and it was not until the Treaty of Peace in
1783 determined that the western country as far as
the Mississippi River was to belong to the United
States that the dammed-up population broke over
the mountains in a veritable flood.

The western country and its people presented no
easy problem to the United States: how to hold
those people when the pull was strong to draw them
from the Union; how to govern citizens so widely
separated from the older communities; and, of
most immediate importance, how to hold the
land itself.   It was, indeed, the question of the
ownership of the land beyond the mountains which

delayed the ratification of the Articles of Confederation. Some of the States, by right of their colonial charter grants "from sea to sea," were claiming large parts of the western region. Other States, whose boundaries were fixed, could put forward no such claims; and, as they were therefore limited in their area of expansion, they were fearful lest in the future they should be overbalanced by those States which might obtain extensive property in the West. It was maintained that the Proclamation of 1763 had changed this western territory into "Crown lands," and as, by the Treaty of Peace, the title had passed to the United States, the non-claimant States had demanded in self-defense that the western land should belong to the country as a whole and not to the individual States. Rhode Island, Maryland, and Delaware were most seriously affected, and they were insistent upon this point. Rhode Island and at length Delaware gave in, so that by February, 1779, Maryland alone held out. In May of that year the instructions of Maryland to her delegates were read in Congress, positively forbidding them to ratify the plan of union unless they should receive definite assurances that the western country would become the common property of the United States. As the consent of all of the Thirteen States was necessary to the establishment of the Confederation, this refusal of Maryland brought matters to a crisis. The question was eagerly discussed, and early in 1780 the deadlock was broken by the action of New York in authorizing her representatives to cede her entire claim in western lands to the United States.

It matters little that the claim of New York was not as good as that of some of the other States, especially that of Virginia. The whole situation was changed. It was no longer necessary for Maryland to defend her position; but the claimant States were compelled to justify themselves before the country for not following New York's example. Congress wisely refrained from any assertion of jurisdiction, and only urgently recommended that States having claims to western lands should cede them in order that the one obstacle to the final ratification of the Articles of Confederation might be removed.

Without much question Virginia's claim was the strongest; but the pressure was too great even for her, and she finally yielded, ceding to the United States, upon certain conditions, all her lands northwest of the Ohio River. Then the Maryland delegates were empowered to ratify the Articles of

Confederation.   This was early in 1781, and in a very short time the other States had followed the example of New York and Virginia.   Certain of the conditions imposed by Virginia were not acceptable to Congress, and three years later, upon specific request, that State withdrew the objectionable conditions and made the cession absolute.

The territory thus ceded, north and west of the Ohio River, constituted the public domain.   Its boundaries were somewhat indefinite, but subsequent surveys confirmed the rough estimate that it contained from one to two hundred millions of acres.   It was supposed to be worth, on the average, about a dollar an acre, which would make this property an asset sufficient to meet the debts of the war and to leave a balance for the running expenses of the Government.   It thereby became one of the strong bonds holding the Union together.

"Land!" was the first cry of the storm-tossed mariners of Columbus.   For three centuries the leading fact of American history has been that soon after 1600 a body of Europeans, mostly Englishmen, settled on the edge of the greatest piece of unoccupied agricultural land in the temperate zone, and proceeded to subdue it to the uses of man.   For three centuries the chief task of American mankind has been to go up westward against the land and to possess it. **Our** wars, our independence, our state building, our political democracy, our plasticity with respect to immigration, our mobility of thought, our ardor of initiative, our mildness and our prosperity, all are but incidents or products of this prime historical fact.[1]

It is seldom that one's attention is so caught and held as by the happy suggestion that American interest in land — or rather interest in American land — began with the discovery of the continent. Even a momentary consideration of the subject, however, is sufficient to indicate how important was the desire for land as a motive of colonization. The foundation of European governmental and social organizations had been laid in feudalism — a system of land-holding and service. And although European states might have lost their original feudal character, and although new classes had arisen, land-holding still remained the basis of social distinction.

One can readily imagine that America would be considered as El Dorado, where one of the rarest commodities as well as one of the most precious possessions was found in almost unlimited quantities and could be had for the asking. It is no wonder

[1] Lecture by J. Franklin Jameson before the Trustees of the Carnegie Institution, at Washington, in 1912, printed in the *History Teacher's Magazine*, vol. iv, 1913, p. 5.

that family estates were sought in America and that to the lower classes it seemed as if a heaven were opening on earth. Even though available land appeared to be almost unlimited in quantity and easy to acquire, it was a possession that was generally increasing in value. Of course wasteful methods of farming wore out some lands, especially in the South; but, taking it by and large throughout the country, with time and increasing density of population the value of the land was increasing. The acquisition of land was a matter of investment or at least of speculation. In fact, the purchase of land was one of the favorite get-rich-quick schemes of the time. George Washington was not the only man who invested largely in western lands. A list of those who did would read like a political or social directory of the time. Patrick Henry, James Wilson, Robert Morris, Gouverneur Morris, Chancellor Kent, Henry Knox, and James Monroe were among them.[1]

It is therefore easy to understand why so much importance attached to the claims of the several States and to the cession of that western land by

[1] Not all the speculators were able to keep what they acquired. Fifteen million acres of land in Kentucky were offered for sale in 1800 for non-payment of taxes. Channing, *History of the United States*, vol. iv, p. 91.

them to the United States.   But something more was necessary.   If the land was to attain anything like its real value, settlers must be induced to occupy it.   Of course it was possible to let the people go out as they pleased and take up land, and to let the Government collect from them as might be possible at a fixed rate.   But experience during colonial days had shown the weakness of such a method, and Congress was apparently determined to keep under its own control the region which it now possessed, to provide for orderly sale, and to permit settlement only so far as it might not endanger the national interests.   The method of land sales and the question of government for the western country were recognized as different aspects of the same problem.   The Virginia offer of cession forced the necessity of a decision, and no sooner was the Virginia offer framed in an acceptable form, in 1783, than two committees were appointed by Congress to report upon these two questions of land sales and of government.

Thomas Jefferson was made chairman of both these committees.   He was then forty years old and one of the most remarkable men in the country. Born on the frontier — his father from the upper middle class, his mother "a Randolph" — he had been trained to an outdoor life; but he was also a prodigy in his studies and entered William and Mary College with advanced standing at the age of eighteen.   Many stories are told of his precocity and ability, all of which tend to forecast the later man of catholic tastes, omnivorous interest, and extensive but superficial knowledge; he was a strange combination of natural aristocrat and theoretical democrat, of philosopher and practical politician. After having been a student in the law office of George Wythe, and being a friend of Patrick Henry, Jefferson early espoused the cause of the Revolution, and it was his hand that drafted the Declaration of Independence.   He then resigned from Congress to assist in the organization of government in his own State.   For two years and a half he served in the Virginia Assembly and brought about the repeal of the law of entailment, the abolition of primogeniture, the recognition of freedom of conscience, and the encouragement of education.   He was Governor of Virginia for two years and then, having declined reëlection, returned to Congress in 1783.   There, among his other accomplishments, as chairman of the committee, he reported the Treaty of Peace and, as chairman of another committee, devised and persuaded Congress to adopt a national system of coinage which in its essentials is still in use.

It is easy to criticize Jefferson and to pick flaws in the things that he said as well as in the things that he did, but practically every one admits that he was closely in touch with the course of events and understood the temper of his contemporaries. In this period of transition from the old order to the new, he seems to have expressed the genius of American institutions better than almost any other man of his generation. He possessed a quality that enabled him, in the Declaration of Independence, to give voice to the hopes and aspirations of a rising nationality and that enabled him in his own State to bring about so many reforms.

Just how much actual influence Thomas Jefferson had in the framing of the American land policy is not clear. Although the draft of the committee report in 1784 is in Jefferson's handwriting, it is altogether probable that more credit is to be given to Thomas Hutchins, the Geographer of the United States, and to William Grayson of Virginia, especially for the final form which the measure took; for Jefferson retired from the chairmanship and had already gone to Europe when the Land Ordinance was adopted by Congress in 1785. This ordinance has been superseded by later enactments, to which references are usually made; but the original ordinance is one of the great pieces of American legislation, for it contained the fundamentals of the American land system which, with the modifications experience has introduced, has proved to be permanently workable and which has been envied and in several instances copied by other countries. Like almost all successful institutions of that sort, the Land Ordinance of 1785 was not an immediate creation but was a development out of former practices and customs and was in the nature of a compromise. Its essential features were the method of survey and the process for the sale of land. New England, with its town system, had in the course of its expansion been accustomed to proceed in an orderly method but on a relatively small scale. The South, on the other hand, had granted lands on a larger scale and had permitted individual selection in a haphazard manner. The plan which Congress adopted was that of the New England survey with the Southern method of extensive holdings. The system is repellent in its rectangular orderliness, but it made the process of recording titles easy and complete, and it was capable of indefinite expansion. These were matters of cardinal importance, for in the course of one hundred and forty years the United States was to have under its control nearly two thousand million acres of land.

The primary feature of the land policy was the orderly survey in advance of sale. In the next place the township was taken as the unit, and its size was fixed at six miles square. Provision was then made for the sale of townships alternately entire and by sections of one mile square, or 640 acres each. In every township a section was reserved for educational purposes; that is, the land was to be disposed of and the proceeds used for the development of public schools in that region. And, finally, the United States reserved four sections in the center of each township to be disposed of at a later time. It was expected that a great increase in the value of the land would result, and it was proposed that the Government should reap a part of the profits.

It is evident that the primary purpose of the public land policy as first developed was to acquire revenue for the Government; but it was also evident that there was a distinct purpose of encouraging settlement. The two were not incompatible, but the greater interest of the Government was in obtaining a return for the property.

The other committee of which Jefferson was chairman made its report of a plan for the government of the western territory upon the very day that the Virginia cession was finally accepted, March 1, 1784; and with some important modifications Jefferson's ordinance, or the Ordinance of 1784 as it was commonly called, was ultimately adopted.   In this case Jefferson rendered a service similar to that of framing the Declaration of Inpendence.   His plan was somewhat theoretical and visionary, but largely practical, and it was constructive work of a high order, displaying not so much originality as sympathetic appreciation of what had already been done and an instinctive forecast of future development.   Jefferson seemed to be able to gather up ideas, some conscious and some latent in men's minds, and to express them in a form that was generally acceptable.

It is interesting to find in the Articles of Confederation (Article XI) that, "Canada acceding to this confederation, and joining in the measures of the United States, shall be admitted into, and entitled to all the advantages of this Union: but no other colony shall be admitted into the same unless such admission be agreed to by nine States."   The real importance of this article lay in the suggestion of an enlargement of the Confederation. The Confederation was never intended to be a union of only thirteen States. Before the cession of their western claims it seemed to be inevitable that some of the States should be broken up into several units. At the very time that the formation of the Confederation was under discussion Vermont issued a declaration of independence from New York and New Hampshire, with the expectation of being admitted into the Union. It was impolitic to recognize the appeal at that time, but it seems to have been generally understood that sooner or later Vermont would come in as a full-fledged State.

It might have been a revolutionary suggestion by Maryland, when the cession of western lands was under discussion, that Congress should have sole power to fix the western boundaries of the States, but her further proposal was not even regarded as radical, that Congress should "lay out the land beyond the boundaries so ascertained into separate and independent states." It seems to have been taken as a matter of course in the procedure of Congress and was accepted by the States. But the idea was one thing; its carrying out was quite another. Here was a great extent of western territory which would be valuable only as it could

be sold to prospective settlers. One of the first
things these settlers would demand was protection
— protection against the Indians, possibly also
against the British and the Spanish, and protection
in their ordinary civil life. The former was a detail of military organization and was in due time
provided by the establishment of military forts
and garrisons; the latter was the problem which
Jefferson's committee was attempting to solve.

The Ordinance of 1784 disregarded the natural
physical features of the western country and, by
degrees of latitude and meridians of longitude, ar-
bitrarily divided the public domain into rectangular districts, to the first of which the following
names were applied: Sylvania, Michigania, Cherronesus, Assenisipia, Metropotamia, Illinoia, Sara-
toga, Washington, Polypotamia, Pelisipia. The
amusement which this absurd and thoroughly Jef-
fersonian nomenclature is bound to cause ought not
to detract from the really important features of the
Ordinance. In each of the districts into which the
country was divided the settlers might be authorized by Congress, for the purpose of establishing a
temporary government, to adopt the constitution
and laws of any one of the original States. When
any such area should have twenty thousand free

inhabitants it might receive authority from Congress to establish a permanent constitution and government and should be entitled to a representative in Congress with the right of debating but not of voting. And finally, when the inhabitants of any one of these districts should equal in number those of the least populous of the thirteen original States, their delegates should be admitted into Congress on an equal footing.

Jefferson's ordinance, though adopted, was never put into operation. Various explanations have been offered for this failure to give it a fair trial. It has been said that Jefferson himself was to blame. In the original draft of his ordinance Jefferson had provided for the abolition of slavery in the new States after the year 1800, and when Congress refused to accept this clause Jefferson, in a manner quite characteristic, seemed to lose all interest in the plan. There were, however, other objections, for there were those who felt that it was somewhat indefinite to promise admission into the Confederation of certain sections of the country as soon as their population should equal in number that of the least populous of the original States. If the original States should increase in population to any extent, the new States might never be admitted.

But on the other hand, if from any cause the population of one of the smaller States should suddenly decrease, might not the resulting influx of new States prove dangerous?

But the real reason why the ordinance remained a dead letter was that, while it fixed the limits within which local governments might act, it left the creation of those governments wholly to the future. At Vincennes, for example, the ordinance made no change in the political habits of the people. "The local government bowled along merrily under this system. There was the greatest abundance of government, for the more the United States neglected them the more authority their officials assumed."[1] Nor could the ordinance operate until settlers became numerous. It was partly, indeed, to hasten settlement that the Ordinance of 1785 for the survey and sale of the public lands was passed.[2]

In the meantime efforts were being made by Congress to improve the unsatisfactory ordinance for the government of the West. Committees were

[1] Jacob Piat Dunn, Jr., *Indiana: A Redemption from Slavery*, 1888.

[2] Although the machinery was set in motion, by the appointment of men and the beginning of work, it was not until 1789 that the survey of the first seven ranges of townships was completed and the land offered for sale.

appointed, reports were made, and at intervals of weeks or months the subject was considered. Some amendments were actually adopted, but Congress, notoriously inefficient, hesitated to undertake a fundamental revision of the ordinance. Then, suddenly, in July, 1787, after a brief period of adjournment, Congress took up this subject and within a week adopted the now famous Ordinance of 1787.

The stimulus which aroused Congress to activity seems to have come from the Ohio Company. From the very beginning of the public domain there was a strong sentiment in favor of using western land for settlement by Revolutionary soldiers. Some of these lands had been offered as bounties to encourage enlistment, and after the war the project of soldiers' settlement in the West was vigorously agitated. The Ohio Company of Associates was made up of veterans of the Revolution, who were looking for homes in the West, and of other persons who were willing to support a worthy cause by a subscription which might turn out to be a good investment. The company wished to buy land in the West, and Congress had land which it wished to sell. Under such circumstances it was easy to strike a bargain. The land, as we have seen, was roughly estimated at one dollar an acre; but, as the company wished to purchase a million acres, it demanded and obtained wholesale rates of two-thirds of the usual price.   It also obtained the privilege of paying at least a portion in certificates of Revolutionary indebtedness, some of which were worth about twelve and a half cents on the dollar.   Only a little calculation is required to show that a large quantity of land was therefore sold at about eight or nine cents an acre.   It was in connection with this land sale that the Ordinance of 1787 was adopted.

The promoter of this enterprise undertaken by the Ohio Company was Manasseh Cutler of Ipswich, Massachusetts, a clergyman by profession who had served as a chaplain in the Revolutionary War.   But his interests and activities extended far beyond the bounds of his profession. When the people of his parish were without proper medical advice he applied himself to the study and practice of medicine.   At about the same time he took up the study of botany, and because of his describing several hundred species of plants he is regarded as the pioneer botanist of New England.   His next interest seems to have grown out of his Revolutionary associations, for it centered in this project for settlement of the West, and he was appointed the agent of the Ohio Company. It was in this capacity that he had come to New York and made the bargain with Congress which has just been described. Cutler must have been a good lobbyist, for Congress was not an efficient body, and unremitting labor, as well as diplomacy, was required for so large and important a matter. Two things indicate his method of procedure. In the first place he found it politic to drop his own candidate for the governorship of the new territory and to endorse General Arthur St. Clair, then President of Congress. And in the next place he accepted the suggestion of Colonel William Duer for the formation of another company, known as the Scioto Associates, to purchase five million acres of land on similar terms, "but that it should be kept a profound secret." It was not an accident that Colonel Duer was Secretary of the Board of the Treasury through whom these purchases were made, nor that associated with him in this speculation were "a number of the principal characters in the city." These land deals were completed afterwards, but there is little doubt that there was a direct connection between them and the adoption of the ordinance of government.

The Ordinance of 1787 was so successful in its working and its renown became so great that claims of authorship, even for separate articles, have been filed in the name of almost every person who had the slightest excuse for being considered. Thousands of pages have been written in eulogy and in dispute, to the helpful clearing up of some points and to the obscuring of others. But the authorship of this or of that clause is of much less importance than the scope of the document as a working plan of government. As such the Ordinance of 1787 owes much to Jefferson's Ordinance of 1784. Under the new ordinance a governor and three judges were to be appointed who, along with their other functions, were to select such laws as they thought best from the statute books of all the States. The second stage in self-government would be reached when the population contained five thousand free men of age; then the people were to have a representative legislature with the usual privilege of making their own laws. Provision was made for dividing the whole region northwest of the Ohio River into three or four or five districts and the final stage of government was reached when any one of these districts had sixty thousand free inhabitants, for it might then establish its own constitution and government and be admitted into the Union on an equal footing with the original States.

The last-named provision for admission into the Union, being in the nature of a promise for the future, was not included in the body of the document providing for the government, but was contained in certain "articles of compact, between the original States and the people and States in the said territory, [which should] forever remain unalterable, unless by common consent." These articles of compact were in general similar to the bills of rights in State Constitutions; but one of them found no parallel in any State Constitution. Article VI reads: "There shall be neither slavery nor involuntary servitude in the said territory, otherwise than in the punishment of crimes, whereof the party shall have been duly convicted." This has been hailed as a farsighted, humanitarian measure, and it is quite true that many of the leading men, in the South as well as in the North, were looking forward to the time when slavery would be abolished. But the motives predominating at the time were probably more nearly represented by Grayson, who wrote to James Monroe, three weeks after the ordinance was passed: "The clause respecting slavery was agreed to by the southern members for the purpose of preventing tobacco and indigo from being made on the northwest side of the Ohio, as well as for several other political reasons."

It is now approaching two hundred years since the Ordinance of 1787 was adopted, during which period more than thirty territories of the United States have been organized, and there has never been a time when one or more territories were not under Congressional supervision, so that the process of legislative control has been continuous. Changes have been made from time to time in order to adapt the territorial government to changed conditions, but for fifty years the Ordinance of 1787 actually remained in operation, and even twenty years later it was specifically referred to by statute. The principles of territorial government today are identical with those of 1787, and those principles comprise the largest measure of local self-government compatible with national control, a gradual extension of self-government to the people of a territory, and finally complete statehood and admission into the Union on a footing of equality with the other States.

In 1825, when the military occupation of Oregon

was suggested in Congress, Senator Dickerson
of New Jersey objected, saying, "We have not
adopted a system of colonization and it is to be
hoped we never shall." Yet that is just what
America has always had. Not only were the
first settlers on the Atlantic coast colonists from
Europe; but the men who went to the frontier were
also colonists from the Atlantic seaboard. And
the men who settled the States in the West were
colonists from the older communities. The Americans had so recently asserted their independence
that they regarded the name of colony as not
merely indicating dependence but as implying
something of inferiority and even of reproach.
And when the American colonial system was being
formulated in 1783–87 the word "Colony" was not
used. The country under consideration was the
region west of the Alleghany Mountains and in
particular the territory north and west of the Ohio
River and, being so referred to in the documents,
the word "Territory" became the term applied to
all the colonies.

The Northwest Territory increased so rapidly in
population that in 1800 it was divided into two
districts, and in 1802 the eastern part was admitted
into the Union as the State of Ohio. The rest of

the territory was divided in 1805 and again in 1809; Indiana was admitted as a State in 1816 and Illinois in 1818. So the process has gone on. There were thirteen original States and six more have become members of the Union without having been through the status of territories, making nineteen in all; while thirty-one States have developed from the colonial stage. The incorporation of the colonies into the Union is not merely a political fact; the inhabitants of the colonies become an integral part of the parent nation and in turn become the progenitors of new colonies. If such a process be long continued, the colonies will eventually outnumber the parent States, and the colonists will outnumber the citizens of the original States and will themselves become the nation. Such has been the history of the United States and its people. By 1850, indeed, one-half of the population of the United States was living west of the Alleghany Mountains, and at the present time approximately sixty per cent are to be found in the West.

The importance of the Ordinance of 1787 was hardly overstated by Webster in his famous debate with Hayne when he said: "We are accustomed . . . to praise the lawgivers of antiquity; we help to perpetuate the fame of Solon and Lycurgus;

but I doubt whether one single law of any lawgiver, ancient or modern, has produced effects of more distinct, marked and lasting character than the Ordinance of 1787." While improved means of communication and many other material ties have served to hold the States of the Union together, the political bond was supplied by the Ordinance of 1787, which inaugurated the American colonial system.

CHAPTER V

DARKNESS BEFORE DAWN

JOHN FISKE summed up the prevailing impression of the government of the Confederation in the title to his volume, *The Critical Period of American History*. "The period of five years," says Fiske, "following the peace of 1783 was the most critical moment in all the history of the American people. The dangers from which we were saved in 1788 were even greater than were the dangers from which we were saved in 1865." Perhaps the plight of the Confederation was not so desperate as he would have us believe, but it was desperate enough. Two incidents occurring between the signing of the preliminary terms of peace and the definitive treaty reveal the danger in which the country stood. The main body of continental troops made up of militiamen and short-term volunteers — always prone to mutinous conduct — was collected at Newburg on the Hudson, watching the British in New York.

Word might come at any day that the treaty had been signed, and the army did not wish to be disbanded until certain matters had been settled — primarily the question of their pay.   The officers had been promised half-pay for life, but nothing definite had been done toward carrying out the promise.   The soldiers had no such hope to encourage them, and their pay was sadly in arrears.   In December, 1782, the officers at Newburg drew up an address in behalf of themselves and their men and sent it to Congress.   Therein they made the threat, thinly veiled, of taking matters into their own hands unless their grievances were redressed.

There is reason to suppose that back of this movement — or at least in sympathy with it — were some of the strongest men in civil as in military life, who, while not fomenting insurrection, were willing to bring pressure to bear on Congress and the States.   Congress was unable or unwilling to act, and in March, 1783, a second paper, this time anonymous, was circulated urging the men not to disband until the question of pay had been settled and recommending a meeting of officers on the following day.   If Washington's influence was not counted upon, it was at least hoped that he would not interfere; but as soon as he learned of

what had been done he issued general orders calling
for a meeting of officers on a later day, thus super-
seding the irregular meeting that had been suggested.   On the day appointed the Commander-
in-Chief appeared and spoke with so much warmth
and feeling that his "little address . . . drew
tears from many of the officers."   He inveighed
against the unsigned paper and against the methods that were talked of, for they would mean the
disgrace of the army, and he appealed to the patriotism of the officers, promising his best efforts in
their behalf.   The effect was so strong that, when
Washington withdrew, resolutions were adopted
unanimously expressing their loyalty and their
faith in the justice of Congress and denouncing the
anonymous circular.

The general apprehension was not diminished
by another incident in June.   Some eighty troops
of the Pennsylvania line in camp at Lancaster
marched to Philadelphia and drew up before the
State House, where Congress was sitting.   Their
purpose was to demand better treatment and the
payment of what was owed to them.   So far it
was an orderly demonstration, although not in
keeping with military regulations; in fact the men
had broken away from camp under the lead of

noncommissioned officers.   But when they had been stimulated by drink the disorder became serious. The humiliating feature of the situation was that Congress could do nothing, even in self-protection. They appealed to the Pennsylvania authorities and, when assistance was refused, the members of Congress in alarm fled in the night and three days later gathered in the college building in Princeton.

Congress became the butt of many jokes, but men could not hide the chagrin they felt that their Government was so weak.   The feeling deepened into shame when the helplessness of Congress was displayed before the world.   Weeks and even months passed before a quorum could be obtained to ratify the treaty recognizing the independence of the United States and establishing peace.   Even after the treaty was supposed to be in force the States disregarded its provisions and Congress could do nothing more than utter ineffective protests.   But, most humiliating of all, the British maintained their military posts within the northwestern territory ceded to the United States, and Congress could only request them to retire.   The Americans' pride was hurt and their pockets were touched as well, for an important issue at stake was the control of the lucrative fur trade.   So resentment grew into anger; but the British held on, and the United States was powerless to make them withdraw. To make matters worse, the Confederation, for want of power to levy taxes, was facing bankruptcy, and Congress was unable to devise ways and means to avert a crisis.

The Second Continental Congress had come into existence in 1775. It was made up of delegations from the various colonies, appointed in more or less irregular ways, and had no more authority than it might assume and the various colonies were willing to concede; yet it was the central body under which the Revolution had been inaugurated and carried through to a successful conclusion. Had this Congress grappled firmly with the financial problem and forced through a system of direct taxation, the subsequent woes of the Confederation might have been mitigated and perhaps averted. In their enthusiasm over the Declaration of Independence the people — by whom is meant the articulate class consisting largely of the governing and commercial elements — would probably have accepted such a usurpation of authority. But with their lack of experience it is not surprising that the delegates to Congress did not appreciate the necessity of such radical action and so were unwilling to take the responsibility for it. They counted upon the good-will and support of their constituents, which simmered down to a reliance upon voluntary grants from the States in response to appeals from Congress. These desultory grants proved to be so unsatisfactory that, in 1781, even before the Articles of Confederation had been ratified, Congress asked for a grant of additional power to levy a duty of five per cent *ad valorem* upon all goods imported into the United States, the revenue from which was to be applied to the discharge of the principal and interest on debts "contracted . . . for supporting the present war." Twelve States agreed, but Rhode Island, after some hesitation, finally rejected the measure in November, 1782.

The Articles of Confederation authorized a system of requisitions apportioned among the "several States in proportion to the value of all land within each State." But, as there was no power vested in Congress to force the States to comply, the situation was in no way improved when the Articles were ratified and put into operation. In fact, matters grew worse as Congress itself steadily lost ground in popular estimation, until it had become little better than a laughing-stock, and with the ending of the war its requests were more honored in the breach than in the observance. In 1782 Congress asked for $8,000,000 and the following year for $2,-000,000 more, but by the end of 1783 less than $1,500,000 had been paid in.

In the same year, 1783, Congress made another attempt to remedy the financial situation by proposing the so-called Revenue Amendment, according to which a specific duty was to be laid upon certain articles and a general duty of five per cent *ad valorem* upon all other goods, to be in operation for twenty-five years. In addition to this it was proposed that for the same period of time $1,500,-000 annually should be raised by requisitions, and the definite amount for each State was specified until "the rule of the Confederation" could be carried into practice. It was then proposed that the article providing for the proportion of requisitions should be changed so as to be based not upon land values but upon population, in estimating which slaves should be counted at three-fifths of their number. In the course of three years thereafter only two States accepted the proposals in full, seven agreed to them in part, and four failed to act at all. Congress in despair then made a further representation to the States upon the critical condition of the finances and accompanied this with an urgent appeal, which resulted in all the States except New York agreeing to the proposed impost. But the refusal of one State was sufficient to block the whole measure, and there was no further hope for a treasury that was practically bankrupt. In five years Congress had received less than two and one-half million dollars from requisitions, and for the fourteen months ending January 1, 1786, the income was at the rate of less than $375,000 a year, which was not enough, as a committee of Congress reported, "for the bare maintenance of the Federal Government on the most economical establishment and in time of profound peace." In fact, the income was not sufficient even to meet the interest on the foreign debt.

In the absence of other means of obtaining funds Congress had resorted early to the unfortunate expedient of issuing paper money based solely on the good faith of the States to redeem it. This fiat money held its value for some little time; then it began to shrink and, once started on the downward path, its fall was rapid. Congress tried to meet the emergency by issuing paper in increasing quantities until the inevitable happened: the paper money ceased to have any value and practically disappeared from circulation. Jefferson said that by the end of 1781 one thousand dollars of Continental scrip was worth about one dollar in specie.

The States had already issued paper money of their own, and their experience ought to have taught them a lesson, but with the coming of hard times after the war, they once more proposed by issuing paper to relieve the "scarcity of money" which was commonly supposed to be one of the principal evils of the day. In 1785 and 1786 paper money parties appeared in almost all the States. In some of these the conservative element was strong enough to prevent action, but in others the movement had to run its fatal course. The futility of what they were doing should have been revealed to all concerned by proposals seriously made that the paper money which was issued should depreciate at a regular rate each year until it should finally disappear.

The experience of Rhode Island is not to be regarded as typical of what was happening throughout the country but is, indeed, rather to be considered as exceptional. Yet it attracted widespread attention and revealed to anxious observers the dangers to which the country was subject if the existing condition of affairs were allowed to continue. The machinery of the State Government was captured by the paper-money party in the spring election of 1786. The results were disappointing to the adherents of the paper-money cause, for when the money was issued depreciation began at once, and those who tried to pay their bills discovered that a heavy discount was demanded. In response to indignant demands the legislature of Rhode Island passed an act to force the acceptance of paper money under penalty and thereupon tradesmen refused to make any sales at all — some closed their shops, and others tried to carry on business by exchange of wares. The farmers then retaliated by refusing to sell their produce to the shopkeepers, and general confusion and acute distress followed. It was mainly a quarrel between the farmers and the merchants, but it easily grew into a division between town and country, and there followed a whole series of town meetings and county conventions. The old line of cleavage was fairly well represented by the excommunication of a member of St. John's Episcopal Church of Providence for tendering bank notes, and the expulsion of a member of the Society of the Cincinnati for a similar cause.

The contest culminated in the case of Trevett *vs.* Weeden, 1786, which is memorable in the judicial annals of the United States. The legislature, not being satisfied with ordinary methods of enforcement, had provided for the summary trial of offenders without a jury before a court whose judges were removable by the Assembly and were therefore supposedly subservient to its wishes. In the case in question the Superior Court boldly declared the enforcing act to be unconstitutional, and for their contumacious behavior the judges were summoned before the legislature. They escaped punishment, but only one of them was reëlected to office.

Meanwhile disorders of a more serious sort, which startled the whole country, occurred in Massachusetts. It is doubtful if a satisfactory explanation ever will be found, at least one which will be universally accepted, as to the causes and origin of Shays' Rebellion in 1786. Some historians maintain that the uprising resulted primarily from a scarcity of money, from a shortage in the circulating medium; that, while the eastern counties were keeping up their foreign trade sufficiently at least to bring in enough metallic currency to relieve the stringency and could also use various forms of credit, the western counties had no such remedy. Others are inclined to think that the difficulties of the farmers in western Massachusetts were caused largely by the return to normal conditions after the extraordinarily good times between 1776 and 1780, and that it was the discomfort attending the process that drove them to revolt.   Another explanation reminds one of present-day charges against undue influence of high financial circles, when it is insinuated and even directly charged that the rebellion was fostered by conservative interests who were trying to create a public opinion in favor of a more strongly organized government.

Whatever other causes there may have been, the immediate source of trouble was the enforced payment of indebtedness, which to a large extent had been allowed to remain in abeyance during the war. This postponement of settlement had not been merely for humanitarian reasons; it would have been the height of folly to collect when the currency was greatly depreciated.   But conditions were supposed to have been restored to normal with the cessation of hostilities, and creditors were generally inclined to demand payment.   These demands, coinciding with the heavy taxes, drove the people of western Massachusetts into revolt.   Feeling ran high against lawyers who prosecuted suits for creditors, and this antagonism was easily transferred to the courts in which the suits were brought. The rebellion in Massachusetts accordingly took the form of a demonstration against the courts. A paper was carried from town to town in the County of Worcester, in which the signers promised to do their utmost "to prevent the sitting of the Inferior Court of Common Pleas for the county, or of any other court that should attempt to take property by distress."

The Massachusetts Legislature adjourned in July, 1786, without remedying the trouble and also without authorizing an issue of paper money which the hard-pressed debtors were demanding. In the months following mobs prevented the courts from sitting in various towns. A special session of the legislature was then called by the Governor but, when that special session had adjourned on the 18th of November, it might just as well have never met. It had attempted to remedy various grievances and had made concessions to the malcontents, but it had also passed measures to strengthen the hands of the Governor. This only seemed to inflame the rioters, and the disorders increased. After the lower courts a move was made against the State Supreme Court, and plans were laid for a concerted movement against the cities in the eastern part of the State. Civil war seemed imminent. The insurgents were led by Daniel Shays, an officer in the army of the Revolution, and the party of law and order was represented by Governor James Bowdoin, who raised some four thousand troops and placed them under the command of General Benjamin Lincoln.

The time of year was unfortunate for the insurgents, especially as December was unusually cold and there was a heavy snowfall. Shays could not provide stores and equipment and was unable to maintain discipline. A threatened attack on Cambridge came to naught for, when preparations were made to protect the city, the rebels began a disorderly retreat, and in the intense cold and deep snow they suffered severely, and many died from exposure. The center of interest then shifted to Springfield, where the insurgents were attempting to seize the United States arsenal. The local militia had already repelled the first attacks, and the appearance of General Lincoln with his troops completed the demoralization of Shays' army. The insurgents retreated, but Lincoln pursued relentlessly and broke them up into small bands, which then wandered about the country preying upon the unfortunate inhabitants. When spring came, most of them had been subdued or had taken refuge in the neighboring States.

Shays' Rebellion was fairly easily suppressed, even though it required the shedding of some blood. But it was the possibility of further outbreaks that destroyed men's peace of mind. There were similar disturbances in other States; and there the Massachusetts insurgents found sympathy, support, and finally a refuge. When the worst was over, and Governor Bowdoin applied to the neighboring States for help in capturing the last of the refugees, Rhode Island and Vermont failed to respond to the extent that might have been expected of them. The danger, therefore, of the insurrection spreading was a cause of deep concern. This feeling was increased by the impotence of Congress. The Government had sufficient excuse for intervention after the attack upon the national arsenal in Springfield. Congress, indeed, began to raise troops but did not dare to admit its purpose and offered as a pretext an expedition against the Northwestern Indians. The rebellion was over before any assistance could be given. The inefficiency of Congress and its lack of influence were evident. Like the disorders in Rhode Island, Shays' Rebellion in Massachusetts helped to bring about a reaction and strengthened the conservative movement for reform.

These untoward happenings, however, were only symptoms: the causes of the trouble lay far deeper. This fact was recognized even in Rhode Island, for at least one of the conventions had passed resolutions declaring that, in considering the condition of the whole country, what particularly concerned them was the condition of trade. Paradoxical as it may seem, the trade and commerce of the country were already on the upward grade and prosperity was actually returning. But prosperity is usually a process of slow growth and is seldom recognized by the community at large until it is well established. Farsighted men forecast the coming of good times in advance of the rest of the community, and prosper accordingly. The majority of the people know that prosperity has come only when it is unmistakably present, and some are not aware of it until it has begun to go. If that be true in our day, much more was it true in the eighteenth century, when means of communication were so poor that it took days for a message to go from Boston to New York and weeks for news to get from Boston to Charleston. It was a period of adjustment, and as we look back after the event we can see that the American people were adapting themselves with remarkable skill to the new conditions. But that was not so evident to the men who were feeling the pinch of hard times, and when all the attendant circumstances, some of which have been described, are taken into account, it is not surprising that commercial depression should be one of the strongest influences in, and the immediate occasion of, bringing men to the point of willingness to attempt some radical changes.

The fact needs to be reiterated that the people of the United States were largely dependent upon agriculture and other forms of extractive industry, and that markets for the disposal of their goods were an absolute necessity. Some of the States, especially New England and the Middle States, were interested in the carrying trade, but all were concerned in obtaining markets. On account of jealousy interstate trade continued a precarious existence and by no means sufficed to dispose of the surplus products, so that foreign markets were necessary. The people were especially concerned for the establishment of the old trade with the West India Islands, which had been the mainstay of their prosperity in colonial times; and after the British Government, in 1783, restricted that trade to British vessels, many people in the United States were attributing hard times to British malignancy. The only action which seemed possible was to force Great Britain in particular, but other foreign countries as well, to make such trade agreements as the prosperity of the United States demanded. The only hope seemed to lie in a commercial policy of reprisal which would force other countries to open their markets to American goods. Retaliation was the dominating idea in the foreign policy of the time. So in 1784 Congress made a new recommendation to the States, prefacing it with an assertion of the importance of commerce, saying: "The fortune of every Citizen is interested in the success thereof; for it is the constant source of wealth and incentive to industry; and the value of our produce and our land must ever rise or fall in proportion to the prosperous or adverse state of trade."

And after declaring that Great Britain had "adopted regulations destructive of our commerce with her West India Islands," it was further asserted: "Unless the United States in Congress assembled shall be vested with powers competent to the protection of commerce, they can never command reciprocal advantages in trade." It was therefore proposed to give to Congress for fifteen years the power to prohibit the importation or exportation of goods at American ports except in vessels owned by the people of the United States or by the subjects of foreign governments having treaties of commerce with the United States. This was simply a request for authorization to adopt navigation acts. But the individual States were too much concerned with their own interests and did not or would not appreciate the rights of the other States or the interests of the Union as a whole. And so the commercial amendment of 1784 suffered the fate of all other amendments proposed to the Articles of Confederation. In fact only two States accepted it.

It usually happens that some minor occurrence, almost unnoticed at the time, leads directly to the most important consequences. And an incident in domestic affairs started the chain of events in the United States that ended in the reform of the Federal Government. The rivalry and jealousy among the States had brought matters to such a pass that either Congress must be vested with adequate powers or the Confederation must collapse. But the Articles of Confederation provided no remedy, and it had been found that amendments to that instrument could not be obtained. It was necessary, therefore, to proceed in some extra-legal fashion. The Articles of Confederation specifically forbade treaties or alliances between the States unless approved by Congress. Yet Virginia and Maryland, in 1785, had come to a working agreement regarding the use of the Potomac River, which was the boundary line between them. Commissioners representing both parties had met at Alexandria and soon adjourned to Mount Vernon, where they not only reached an amicable settlement of the immediate questions before them but also discussed the larger subjects of duties and commercial matters in general. When the Maryland legislature came to act on the report, it proposed that Pennsylvania and Delaware should be invited to join with them in formulating a common commercial policy. Virginia then went one step farther and invited all the other States to send commissioners to a general trade convention and later announced Annapolis as the place of meeting and set the time for September, 1786.

This action was unconstitutional and was so recognized, for James Madison notes that "from the Legislative Journals of Virginia it appears, that a vote to apply for a sanction of Congress was followed by a vote against a communication of the Compact to Congress," and he mentions other similar violations of the central authority. That this did not attract more attention was probably due to the public interest being absorbed just at that time by the paper money agitation. Then, too, the men concerned seem to have been willing to avoid publicity. Their purposes are well brought out in a letter of Monsieur Louis Otto, French Chargé d'Affaires, written on October 10, 1786, to the Comte de Vergennes, Minister for Foreign Affairs, though their motives may be somewhat misinterpreted.

Although there are no nobles in America, there is a class of men denominated "gentlemen," who, by reason of their wealth, their talents, their education, their families, or the offices they hold, aspire to a preeminence which the people refuse to grant them; and, although many of these men have betrayed the interests of their order to gain popularity, there reigns among them a connection so much the more intimate as they almost all of them dread the efforts of the people to despoil them of their possessions, and, moreover, they are creditors, and therefore interested in strengthening the government, and watching over the execution of the laws.

These men generally pay very heavy taxes, while the small proprietors escape the vigilance of the collectors.

The majority of them being merchants, it is for their interest to establish the credit of the United States in Europe on a solid foundation by the exact payment of debts, and to grant to congress powers extensive enough to compel the people to contribute for this purpose. The attempt, my lord, has been vain, by pamphlets and other publications, to spread notions of justice and integrity, and to deprive the people of a freedom which they have so misused. By proposing a new organization of the federal government all minds would have been revolted; circumstances ruinous to the commerce of America have happily arisen to furnish the reformers with a pretext for introducing innovations.

They represented to the people that the American name had become opprobrious among all the nations of Europe; that the flag of the United States was everywhere exposed to insults and annoyance; the husbandman, no longer able to export his produce freely, would soon be reduced to want; it was high time to retaliate, and to convince foreign powers that the United States would not with impunity suffer such a violation of the freedom of trade, but that strong measures could be taken only with the consent of the thirteen states, and that congress, not having the necessary powers, it was essential to form a general assembly instructed to present to congress the plan for its adoption, and to point out the means of carrying it into execution.

The people, generally discontented with the obstacles in the way of commerce, and scarcely suspecting the secret motives of their opponents, ardently embraced this measure, and appointed commissioners, who were to assemble at Annapolis in the beginning of September.

The authors of this proposition had no hope, nor even desire, to see the success of this assembly of commissioners, which was only intended to prepare a question much more important than that of commerce. The measures were so well taken that at the end of September no more than five states were represented at Annapolis, and the commissioners from the northern states tarried several days at New York in order to retard their arrival.

The states which assembled, after having waited nearly three weeks, separated under the pretext that they were not in sufficient numbers to enter on business, and, to justify this dissolution, they addressed to the different legislatures and to congress a report, the translation of which I have the honor to enclose to you.[1]

Among these "men denominated 'gentlemen'" to whom the French Chargé d'Affaires alludes, was James Madison of Virginia. He was one of the younger men, unfitted by temperament and physique to be a soldier, who yet had found his opportunity in the Revolution. Graduating in 1771 from Princeton, where tradition tells of the part he took in patriotic demonstrations on the campus — characteristic of students then as now — he had thrown himself heart and soul into the American cause. He was a member of the convention to

[1] Quoted by Bancroft, *History of the Formation of the Constitution*, vol. ii, Appendix, pp. 399–400.

frame the first State Constitution for Virginia in 1776, and from that time on, because of his ability, he was an important figure in the political history of his State and of his country. He was largely responsible for bringing about the conference between Virginia and Maryland and for the subsequent steps resulting in the trade convention at Annapolis. And yet Madison seldom took a conspicuous part, preferring to remain in the background and to allow others to appear as the leaders. When the Annapolis Convention assembled, for example, he suffered Alexander Hamilton of New York to play the leading rôle.

Hamilton was then approaching thirty years of age and was one of the ablest men in the United States. Though his best work was done in later years, when he proved himself to be perhaps the most brilliant of American statesmen, with an extraordinary genius for administrative organization, the part that he took in the affairs of this period was important. He was small and slight in person but with an expressive face, fair complexion, and cheeks of "almost feminine rosiness." The usual aspect of his countenance was thoughtful and even severe, but in conversation his face lighted up with a remarkably attractive smile. He carried himself erectly and with dignity, so that in spite of his small figure, when he entered a room "it was apparent, from the respectful attention of the company, that he was a distinguished person." A contemporary, speaking of the opposite and almost irreconcilable traits of Hamilton's character, pronounced a bust of him as giving a complete exposition of his character: "Draw a handkerchief around the mouth of the bust, and the remnant of the countenance represents fortitude and intrepidity such as we have often seen in the plates of Roman heroes. Veil in the same manner the face and leave the mouth and chin only discernible, and all this fortitude melts and vanishes into almost feminine softness."

Hamilton was a leading spirit in the Annapolis Trade Convention and wrote the report that it adopted. Whether or not there is any truth in the assertion of the French chargé that Hamilton and others thought it advisable to disguise their purposes, there is no doubt that the Annapolis Convention was an all-important step in the progress of reform, and its recommendation was the direct occasion of the calling of the great convention that framed the Constitution of the United States.

The recommendation of the Annapolis delegates was in the form of a report to the legislatures of their respective States, in which they referred to the defects in the Federal Government and called for "a convention of deputies from the different states for the special purpose of entering into this investigation and digesting a Plan for supplying such defects." Philadelphia was suggested as the place of meeting, and the time was fixed for the second Monday in May of the next year.

Several of the States acted promptly upon this recommendation and in February, 1787, Congress adopted a resolution accepting the proposal and calling the convention "for the sole and express purpose of revising the Articles of Confederation and reporting . . . such alterations . . . as shall . . . render the Federal Constitution adequate to the exigencies of Government and the preservation of the Union." Before the time fixed for the meeting of the Philadelphia Convention, or shortly after that date, all the States had appointed deputies with the exception of New Hampshire and Rhode Island. New Hampshire was favorably disposed toward the meeting but, owing to local conditions, failed to act before the Convention was well under way. Delegates, however, arrived in time to share in some of the most important proceedings. Rhode Island alone refused to take part, although a letter signed by some of the prominent men was sent to the Convention pledging their support.

CHAPTER VI

THE FEDERAL CONVENTION

THE body of delegates which met in Philadelphia in 1787 was the most important convention that ever sat in the United States. The Confederation was a failure, and if the new nation was to be justified in the eyes of the world, it must show itself capable of effective union. The members of the Convention realized the significance of the task before them, which was, as Madison said, "now to decide forever the fate of Republican government." Gouverneur Morris, with unwonted seriousness, declared: "The whole human race will be affected by the proceedings of this Convention." James Wilson spoke with equal gravity: "After the lapse of six thousand years since the creation of the world America now presents the first instance of a people assembled to weigh deliberately and calmly and to decide leisurely and peaceably upon the form of government by which they will bind themselves and their posterity."

Not all the men to whom this undertaking was entrusted, and who were taking themselves and their work so seriously, could pretend to social distinction, but practically all belonged to the upper ruling class. At the Indian Queen, a tavern on Fourth Street between Market and Chestnut, some of the delegates had a hall in which they lived by themselves. The meetings of the Convention were held in an upper room of the State House. The sessions were secret; sentries were placed at the door to keep away all intruders; and the pavement of the street in front of the building was covered with loose earth so that the noises of passing traffic should not disturb this august assembly. It is not surprising that a tradition grew up about the Federal Convention which hedged it round with a sort of awe and reverence. Even Thomas Jefferson referred to it as "an assembly of demigods." If we can get away from the glamour which has been spread over the work of the Fathers of the Constitution and understand that they were human beings, even as we are, and influenced by the same motives as other men, it may be possible to obtain a more faithful impression of what actually took place.

Since representation in the Convention was to be

by States, just as it had been in the Continental
Congress, the presence of delegations from a majority of the States was necessary for organization.
It is a commentary upon the times, upon the difficulties of travel, and upon the leisurely habits of
the people, that the meeting which had been called
for the 14th of May could not begin its work for
over ten days. The 25th of May was stormy, and
only twenty-nine delegates were on hand when
the Convention organized. The slender attendance
can only partially be attributed to the weather, for
in the following three months and a half of the Convention, at which fifty-five members were present
at one time or another, the average attendance was
only slightly larger than that of the first day.   In
such a small body personality counted for much, in
ways that the historian can only surmise.   Many
compromises of conflicting interests were reached
by informal discussion outside of the formal sessions.   In these small gatherings individual character was often as decisive as weighty argument.

George Washington was unanimously chosen as
the presiding officer of the Convention.   He sat on
a raised platform, in a large, carved, high-backed
chair, from which his commanding figure and dignified bearing exerted a potent influence on the

assembly, an influence enhanced by the formal courtesy and stately intercourse of the times. Washington was the great man of his day and the members not only respected and admired him; some of them were actually afraid of him. When he rose to his feet he was almost the Commander-in-Chief again. There is evidence to show that his support or disapproval was at times a decisive factor in the deliberations of the Convention.

Virginia, which had taken a conspicuous part in the calling of the Convention, was looked to for leadership in the work that was to be done. James Madison, next to Washington the most important member of the Virginia delegation, was the very opposite of Washington in many respects — small and slight in stature, inconspicuous in dress as in figure, modest and retiring, but with a quick, active mind and wide knowledge obtained both from experience in public affairs and from extensive reading. Washington was the man of action; Madison, the scholar in politics. Madison was the younger by nearly twenty years, but Washington admired him greatly and gave him the support of his influence — a matter of no little consequence, for Madison was the leading expert worker of the Convention in the business of framing the Constitution.

Governor Edmund Randolph, with his tall figure, handsome face, and dignified manner, made an excellent impression in the position accorded to him of nominal leader of the Virginia delegation. Among others from the same State who should be noticed were the famous lawyers, George Wythe and George Mason.

Among the deputies from Pennsylvania the foremost was James Wilson, the "Caledonian," who probably stood next in importance in the Convention to Madison and Washington. He had come to America as a young man just when the troubles with England were beginning and by sheer ability had attained a position of prominence. Several times a member of Congress, a signer of the Declaration of Independence, he was now regarded as one of the ablest lawyers in the United States. A more brilliant member of the Pennsylvania delegation, and one of the most brilliant of the Convention, was Gouverneur Morris, who shone by his cleverness and quick wit as well as by his wonderful command of language. But Morris was admired more than he was trusted; and, while he supported the efforts for a strong government, his support was not always as great a help as might have been expected. A crippled arm and a wooden leg might detract from his personal appearance, but they could not subdue his spirit and audacity.[1]

There were other prominent members of the Pennsylvania delegation, but none of them took an important part in the Convention, not even the aged Benjamin Franklin, President of the State. At the age of eighty-one his powers were failing, and he was so feeble that his colleague Wilson read his speeches for him. His opinions were respected, but they do not seem to have carried much weight.

Other noteworthy members of the Convention, though hardly in the first class, were the handsome and charming Rufus King of Massachusetts, one of the coming men of the country, and Nathaniel

---

[1] There is a story which illustrates admirably the audacity of Morris and the austere dignity of Washington. The story runs that Morris and several members of the Cabinet were spending an evening at the President's house in Philadelphia, where they were discussing the absorbing question of the hour, whatever it may have been. "The President," Morris is said to have related on the following day, "was standing with his arms behind him — his usual position — his back to the fire. I started up and spoke, stamping, as I walked up and down, with my wooden leg; and, as I was certain I had the best of the argument, as I finished I stalked up to the President, slapped him on the back, and said, 'Ain't I right, General?' The President did not speak, but the majesty of the American people was before me. Oh, his look! How I wished the floor would open and I could descend to the cellar! You know me," continued Mr. Morris, "and you know my eye would never quail before any other mortal." —W. T. Read, *Life and Correspondence of George Read* (1870) p. 441.

Gorham of the same State, who was President of Congress — a man of good sense rather than of great ability, but one whose reputation was high and whose presence was a distinct asset to the Convention. Then, too, there were the delegates from South Carolina: John Rutledge, the orator, General Charles Cotesworth Pinckney of Revolutionary fame, and his cousin, Charles Pinckney. The last named took a conspicuous part in the proceedings in Philadelphia but, so far as the outcome was concerned, left his mark on the Constitution mainly in minor matters and details.

The men who have been named were nearly all supporters of the plan for a centralized government. On the other side were William Paterson of New Jersey, who had been Attorney-General of his State for eleven years and who was respected for his knowledge and ability; John Dickinson of Delaware, the author of the *Farmer's Letters* and chairman of the committee of Congress that had framed the Articles of Confederation — able, scholarly, and sincere, but nervous, sensitive, and conscientious to the verge of timidity — whose refusal to sign the Declaration of Independence had cost him his popularity, though he was afterward returned to Congress and became president successively of

Delaware and of Pennsylvania; Elbridge Gerry of Massachusetts, a successful merchant, prominent in politics, and greatly interested in questions of commerce and finance; and the Connecticut delegates, forming an unusual trio, Dr. William Samuel Johnson, Roger Sherman, and Oliver Ellsworth. These men were fearful of establishing too strong a government and were at one time or another to be found in opposition to Madison and his supporters. They were not mere obstructionists, however, and while not constructive in the same way that Madison and Wilson were, they must be given some credit for the form which the Constitution finally assumed.   Their greatest service was in restraining the tendency of the majority to overrule the rights of States and in modifying the desires of individuals for a government that would have been too strong to work well in practice.

Alexander Hamilton of New York, as one of the ablest members of the Convention, was expected to take an important part, but he was out of touch with the views of the majority.   He was aristocratic rather than democratic and, however excellent his ideas may have been, they were too radical for his fellow delegates and found but little support.   He threw his strength in favor of a strong government and was ready to aid the movement in whatever way he could. But within his own delegation he was outvoted by Robert Yates and John Lansing, and before the sessions were half over he was deprived of a vote by the withdrawal of his colleagues. Thereupon, finding himself of little service, he went to New York and returned to Philadelphia only once or twice for a few days at a time, and finally to sign the completed document. Luther Martin of Maryland was an able lawyer and the Attorney-General of his State; but he was supposed to be allied with undesirable interests, and it was said that he had been sent to the Convention for the purpose of opposing a strong government. He proved to be a tiresome speaker and his prosiness, when added to the suspicion attaching to his motives, cost him much of the influence which he might otherwise have had.

All in all, the delegates to the Federal Convention were a remarkable body of men. Most of them had played important parts in the drama of the Revolution; three-fourths of them had served in Congress, and practically all were persons of note in their respective States and had held important public positions. They may not have been the "assembly of demigods" which Jefferson called them, for another contemporary insisted "that twenty assemblies of equal number might be collected equally respectable both in point of ability, integrity, and patriotism." Perhaps it would be safer to regard the Convention as a fairly representative body, which was of a somewhat higher order than would be gathered together today, because the social conditions of those days tended to bring forward men of a better class, and because the seriousness of the crisis had called out leaders of the highest type.

Two or three days were consumed in organizing the Convention — electing officers, considering the delegates' credentials, and adopting rules of procedure; and when these necessary preliminaries had been accomplished the main business was opened with the presentation by the Virginia delegation of a series of resolutions providing for radical changes in the machinery of the Confederation. The principal features were the organization of a legislature of two houses proportional to population and with increased powers, the establishment of a separate executive, and the creation of an independent judiciary. This was in reality providing for a new government and was probably quite beyond the ideas of most of the members of the Convention, who had come there under instructions and with the expectation of revising the Articles of Confederation. But after the Virginia Plan had been the subject of discussion for two weeks so that the members had become a little more accustomed to its proposals, and after minor modifications had been made in the wording of the resolutions, the Convention was won over to its support. To check this drift toward radical change the opposition headed by New Jersey and Connecticut presented the so-called New Jersey Plan, which was in sharp contrast to the Virginia Resolutions, for it contemplated only a revision of the Articles of Confederation, but after a relatively short discussion, the Virginia Plan was adopted by a vote of seven States against four, with one State divided.

The dividing line between the two parties or groups in the Convention had quickly manifested itself. It proved to be the same line that had divided the Congress of the Confederation, the cleavage between the large States and the small States. The large States were in favor of representation in both houses of the legislature according to population, while the small States were opposed to any change which would deprive them of their equal vote in Congress, and though outvoted, they were not ready to yield. The Virginia Plan, and subsequently the New Jersey Plan, had first been considered in committee of the whole, and the question of "proportional representation," as it was then called, would accordingly come up again in formal session. Several weeks had been occupied by the proceedings, so that it was now near the end of June, and in general the discussions had been conducted with remarkably good temper. But it was evidently the calm before the storm. And the issue was finally joined when the question of representation in the two houses again came before the Convention. The majority of the States on the 29th of June once more voted in favor of proportional representation in the lower house. But on the question of the upper house, owing to a peculiar combination of circumstances — the absence of one delegate and another's change of vote causing the position of their respective States to be reversed or nullified — the vote on the 2d of July resulted in a tie. This brought the proceedings of the Convention to a standstill. A committee of one member from each State was appointed to consider the question, and, "that time might be given to the Committee, and to such as chose to attend to the celebration on the anniversary of Independence, the Convention adjourned" over the Fourth. The committee was chosen by ballot, and its composition was a clear indication that the small-State men had won their fight, and that a compromise would be effected.

It was during the debate upon this subject, when feeling was running high and when at times it seemed as if the Convention in default of any satisfactory solution would permanently adjourn, that Franklin proposed that "prayers imploring the assistance of Heaven . . . be held in this Assembly every morning." Tradition relates that Hamilton opposed the motion. The members were evidently afraid of the impression which would be created outside, if it were suspected that there were dissensions in the Convention, and the motion was not put to a vote.

How far physical conditions may influence men in adopting any particular course of action it is impossible to say. But just when the discussion in the Convention reached a critical stage, just when the compromise presented by the committee was ready for adoption or rejection, the weather turned from unpleasantly hot to being comfortably cool. And, after some little time spent in the consideration of details, on the 16th of July, the great compromise of the Constitution was adopted. There was no other that compared with it in importance. Its most significant features were that in the upper house each State should have an equal vote and that in the lower house representation should be apportioned on the basis of population, while direct taxation should follow the same proportion. The further proviso that money bills should originate in the lower house and should not be amended in the upper house was regarded by some delegates as of considerable importance, though others did not think so, and eventually the restriction upon amendment by the upper house was dropped.

There has long been a prevailing belief that an essential feature of the great compromise was the counting of only three-fifths of the slaves in enumerating the population. This impression is quite erroneous. It was one of the details of the compromise, but it had been a feature of the revenue amendment of 1783, and it was generally accepted as a happy solution of the difficulty that slaves possessed the attributes both of persons and of property. It had been included both in the amended Virginia Plan and in the New Jersey Plan; and when it was embodied in the compromise it was described as "the ratio recommended by Congress in their resolutions of April 18, 1783." A few months later, in explaining the matter to the Massachusetts convention, Rufus King said that, "This rule . . . was adopted because it was the language of all America." In reality the three-fifths rule was a mere incident in that part of the great compromise which declared that "representation should be proportioned according to direct taxation." As a further indication of the attitude of the Convention upon this point, an amendment to have the Blacks counted equally with the Whites was voted down by eight States against two.

With the adoption of the great compromise a marked difference was noticeable in the attitude of the delegates. Those from the large States were deeply disappointed at the result and they asked for an adjournment to give them time to consider what they should do. The next morning, before the Convention met, they held a meeting to determine upon their course of action. They were apparently afraid of taking the responsibility for breaking up the Convention, so they finally decided to let the proceedings go on and to see what might be the ultimate outcome. Rumors of these dissensions had reached the ears of the public, and it may have been to quiet any misgivings that the following inspired item appeared in several local papers: "So great is the unanimity, we hear, that prevails in the Convention, upon all great federal subjects, that it has been proposed to call the room in which they assemble Unanimity Hall."

On the other hand the effect of this great compromise upon the delegates from the small States was distinctly favorable. Having obtained equal representation in one branch of the legislature, they now proceeded with much greater willingness to consider the strengthening of the central government. Many details were yet to be arranged, and sharp differences of opinion existed in connection with the executive as well as with the judiciary. But these difficulties were slight in comparison with those which they had already surmounted in the matter of representation. By the end of July the fifteen resolutions of the original Virginia Plan had been increased to twenty-three, with many enlargements and amendments, and the Convention had gone as far as it could effectively in determining the general principles upon which the government should be formed. There were too many members to work efficiently when it came to the actual framing of a constitution with all the inevitable details that were necessary in setting up a machinery of government. Accordingly this task was turned over to a committee of five members who had already given evidence of their ability in this direction. Rutledge was made the chairman, and the others were Randolph, Gorham, Ellsworth, and Wilson. To give them time to perfect their work, on the 26th of July the Convention adjourned for ten days.

CHAPTER VII

FINISHING THE WORK

RUTLEDGE and his associates on the committee of detail accomplished so much in such a short time that it seems as if they must have worked day and night. Their efforts marked a distinct stage in the development of the Constitution. The committee left no records, but some of the members retained among their private papers drafts of the different stages of the report they were framing, and we are therefore able to surmise the way in which the committee proceeded. Of course the members were bound by the resolutions which had been adopted by the Convention and they held themselves closely to the general principles that had been laid down. But in the elaboration of details they seem to have begun with the Articles of Confederation and to have used all of that document that was consistent with the new plan of government. Then they made use of the New Jersey Plan, which had been put forward by the smaller States, and of a third plan which had been presented by Charles Pinckney; for the rest they drew largely upon the State Constitutions. By a combination of these different sources the committee prepared a document bearing a close resemblance to the present Constitution, although subjects were in a different order and in somewhat different proportions, which, at the end of ten days, by working on Sunday, they were able to present to the Convention. This draft of a constitution was printed on seven folio pages with wide margins for notes and emendations.

The Convention resumed its sessions on Monday, the 6th of August, and for five weeks the report of the committee of detail was the subject of discussion. For five hours each day, and sometimes for six hours, the delegates kept persistently at their task. It was midsummer, and we read in the diary of one of the members that in all that period only five days were "cool." Item by item, line by line, the printed draft of the Constitution was considered. It is not possible, nor is it necessary, to follow that work minutely; much of it was purely formal, and yet any one who has had experience with committee reports knows how much importance attaches to matters of phrasing. Just as the

Virginia Plan was made more acceptable to the majority by changes in wording that seem to us insignificant, so modifications in phrasing slowly won support for the draft of the Constitution.

The adoption of the great compromise, as we have seen, changed the whole spirit of the Convention. There was now an expectation on the part of the members that something definite was going to be accomplished, and all were concerned in making the result as good and as acceptable as possible. In other words, the spirit of compromise pervaded every action, and it is essential to remember this in considering what was accomplished.

One of the greatest weaknesses of the Confederation was the inefficiency of Congress. More than four pages, or three-fifths of the whole printed draft, were devoted to Congress and its powers. It is more significant, however, that in the new Constitution the legislative powers of the Confederation were transferred bodily to the Congress of the United States, and that the powers added were few in number, although of course of the first importance. The Virginia Plan declared that, in addition to the powers under the Confederation, Congress should have the right "to legislate in all cases to which the separate States are incompetent."

This statement was elaborated in the printed draft which granted specific powers of taxation, of regulating commerce, of establishing a uniform rule of naturalization, and at the end of the enumeration of powers two clauses were added giving to Congress authority:

> To call forth the aid of the militia, in order to execute the laws of the Union, enforce treaties, suppress insurrections, and repel invasions;
>
> And to make all laws that shall be necessary and proper for carrying into execution the foregoing powers.

On the other hand, it was necessary to place some limitations upon the power of Congress. A general restriction was laid by giving to the executive a right of veto, which might be overruled, however, by a two-thirds vote of both houses. Following British tradition — yielding as it were to an inherited fear — these delegates in America were led to place the first restraint upon the exercise of congressional authority in connection with treason. The legislature of the United States was given the power to declare the punishment of treason; but treason itself was defined in the Constitution, and it was further asserted that a person could be convicted of treason only on the testimony of two witnesses, and that attainder of treason should not "work corruption of blood nor forfeiture except during the life of the person attainted." Arising more nearly out of their own experience was the prohibition of export taxes, of capitation taxes, and of the granting of titles of nobility.

While the committee of detail was preparing its report, the Southern members of that committee had succeeded in getting a provision inserted that navigation acts could be passed only by a two-thirds vote of both houses of the legislature. New England and the Middle States were strongly in favor of navigation acts for, if they could require all American products to be carried in American-built and American-owned vessels, they would give a great stimulus to the ship-building and commerce of the United States. They therefore wished to give Congress power in this matter on exactly the same terms that other powers were granted. The South, however, was opposed to this policy, for it wanted to encourage the cheapest method of shipping its raw materials. The South also wanted a larger number of slaves to meet its labor demands. To this need New England was not favorably disposed. To reconcile the conflicting interests of the two sections a compromise was finally reached. The requirement of a two-thirds vote of both houses for the passing of navigation acts which the Southern members had obtained was abandoned, and on the other hand it was determined that Congress should not be allowed to interfere with the importation of slaves for twenty years. This, again, was one of the important and conspicuous compromises of the Constitution. It is liable, however, to be misunderstood, for one should not read into the sentiment of the members of the Convention any of the later strong prejudice against slavery. There were some who objected on moral grounds to the recognition of slavery in the Constitution, and that word was carefully avoided by referring to "such Persons as any States now existing shall think proper to admit." And there were some who were especially opposed to the encouragement of that institution by permitting the slave trade, but the majority of the delegates regarded slavery as an accepted institution, as a part of the established order, and public sentiment on the slave trade was not much more emphatic and positive than it is now on cruelty to animals. As Ellsworth said, "The morality or wisdom of slavery are considerations belonging to the States themselves," and the compromise was nothing more or less than a bargain between the sections.

The fundamental weakness of the Confederation was the inability of the Government to enforce its decrees, and in spite of the increased powers of Congress, even including the use of the militia "to execute the laws of the Union," it was not felt that this defect had been entirely remedied. Experience under the Confederation had taught men that something more was necessary in the direction of restricting the States in matters which might interfere with the working of the central Government. As in the case of the powers of Congress, the Articles of Confederation were again resorted to and the restrictions which had been placed upon the States in that document were now embodied in the Constitution with modifications and additions. But the final touch was given in connection with the judiciary.

There was little in the printed draft and there is comparatively little in the Constitution on the subject of the judiciary. A Federal Supreme Court was provided for, and Congress was permitted, but not required, to establish inferior courts; while the jurisdiction of these tribunals was determined upon the general principles that it should extend to cases arising under the Constitution and laws of the United States, to treaties and cases in which foreigners and foreign countries were involved, and to controversies between States and citizens of different States. Nowhere in the document itself is there any word as to that great power which has been exercised by the Federal courts of declaring null and void laws or parts of laws that are regarded as in contravention to the Constitution. There is little doubt that the more important men in the Convention, such as Wilson, Madison, Gouverneur Morris, King, Gerry, Mason, and Luther Martin, believed that the judiciary would exercise this power, even though it should not be specifically granted. The nearest approach to a declaration of this power is to be found in a paragraph that was inserted toward the end of the Constitution. Oddly enough, this was a modification of a clause introduced by Luther Martin with quite another intent. As adopted it reads: "That this Constitution and the Laws of the United States . . . and all Treaties . . . shall be the supreme Law of the Land; and the Judges in every State shall be bound thereby; any Thing in the Constitution or Laws of any State to the Contrary notwithstanding." This paragraph may well be regarded as the keystone of the constitutional arch of national power. Its significance lies in the fact that the Constitution is regarded not as a treaty nor as an agreement between States, but as a law; and while its enforcement is backed by armed power, it is a law enforceable in the courts.

One whole division of the Constitution has been as yet barely referred to, and it not only presented one of the most perplexing problems which the Convention faced but one of the last to be settled — that providing for an executive. There was a general agreement in the Convention that there should be a separate executive. The opinion also developed quite early that a single executive was better than a plural body, but that was as far as the members could go with any degree of unanimity. At the outset they seemed to have thought that the executive would be dependent upon the legislature, appointed by that body, and therefore more or less subject to its control. But in the course of the proceedings the tendency was to grant greater and greater powers to the executive; in other words, he was becoming a figure of importance. No such office as that of President of the United States was then in existence. It was a new position which they were creating. We have become so accustomed to it that it is difficult for us to hark back to the time when there was no such officer and to realize the difficulties and the fears of the men who were responsible for creating that office.

The presidency was obviously modeled after the governorship of the individual States, and yet the incumbent was to be at the head of the Thirteen States. Rufus King is frequently quoted to the effect that the men of that time had been accustomed to considering themselves subjects of the British king. Even at the time of the Convention there is good evidence to show that some of the members were still agitating the desirability of establishing a monarchy in the United States. It was a common rumor that a son of George III was to be invited to come over, and there is reason to believe that only a few months before the Convention met Prince Henry of Prussia was approached by prominent people in this country to see if he could be induced to accept the headship of the States, that is, to become the king of the United States. The members of the Convention evidently thought that they were establishing something like a monarchy. As Randolph said, the people would see "the form at least of a little monarch," and they did not want him to have despotic powers. When the sessions were over, a lady asked Franklin: "Well, Doctor, what have we got,

a republic or a monarchy?"   "A republic," replied
the doctor, "if you can keep it."

The increase of powers accruing to the executive
office necessitated placing a corresponding check
upon the exercise of those powers.   The obvious
method was to render the executive subject to impeachment, and it was also readily agreed that his
veto might be overruled by a two-thirds vote of
Congress; but some further safeguards were necessary, and the whole question accordingly turned
upon the method of his election and the length of
his term.   In the course of the proceedings of the
Convention, at several different times, the members voted in favor of an appointment by the national legislature, but they also voted against
it.   Once they voted for a system of electors chosen by the State legislatures and twice they voted
against such a system.   Three times they voted to
reconsider the whole question.   It is no wonder
that Gerry should say: "We seem to be entirely
at a loss."

So it came to the end of August, with most of the
other matters disposed of and with the patience of
the delegates worn out by the long strain of four
weeks' close application.   During the discussions it
had become apparent to every one that an election

of the President by the people would give a decided advantage to the large States, so that again there was arising the divergence between the large and small States. In order to hasten matters to a conclusion, this and all other vexing details upon which the Convention could not agree were turned over to a committee made up of a member from each State. It was this committee which pointed the way to a compromise by which the choice of the executive was to be entrusted to electors chosen in each State as its legislature might direct. The electors were to be equal in number to the State's representation in Congress, including both senators and representatives, and in each State they were to meet and to vote for two persons, one of whom should not be an inhabitant of that State. The votes were to be listed and sent to Congress, and the person who had received the greatest number of votes was to be President, provided such a number was a majority of all the electors. In case of a tie the Senate was to choose between the candidates and, if no one had a majority, the Senate was to elect "from the five highest on the list."

This method of voting would have given the large States a decided advantage, of course, in that they would appoint the greater number of electors, but it was not believed that this system would ordinarily result in a majority of votes being cast for one man.   Apparently no one anticipated the formation of political parties which would concentrate the votes upon one or another candidate.   It was rather expected that in the great majority of cases—"nineteen times in twenty," one of the delegates said — there would be several candidates and that the selection from those candidates would fall to the Senate, in which all the States were equally represented and the small States were in the majority.   But since the Senate shared so many powers with the executive, it seemed better to transfer the right of "eventual election" to the House of Representatives, where each State was still to have but one vote.   Had this scheme worked as the designers expected, the interests of large States and small States would have been reconciled, since in effect the large States would name the candidates and, "nineteen times in twenty," the small States would choose from among them.

Apparently the question of a third term was never considered by the delegates in the Convention.   The chief problem before them was the method of election.   If the President was to be chosen by the legislature, he should not be eligible to reëlection. On the other hand, if there was to be some form of popular election, an opportunity for reëlection was thought to be a desirable incentive to good behavior. Six or seven years was taken as an acceptable length for a single term and four years a convenient tenure if reëlection was permitted. It was upon these considerations that the term of four years was eventually agreed upon, with no restriction placed upon reëlection.

When it was believed that a satisfactory method of choosing the President had been discovered — and it is interesting to notice the members of the Convention later congratulated themselves that at least this feature of their government was above criticism — it was decided to give still further powers to the President, such as the making of treaties and the appointing of ambassadors and judges, although the advice and consent of the Senate was required, and in the case of treaties two-thirds of the members present must consent.

The presidency was frankly an experiment, the success of which would depend largely upon the first election; yet no one seems to have been anxious about the first choice of chief magistrate, and the reason is not far to seek. From the moment the members agreed that there should be a single executive they also agreed upon the man for the position. Just as Washington had been chosen unanimously to preside over the Convention, so it was generally accepted that he would be the first head of the new state. Such at least was the trend of conversation and even of debate on the floor of the Convention. It indicates something of the conception of the office prevailing at the time that Washington, when he became President, is said to have preferred the title, "His High Mightiness, the President of the United States and Protector of their Liberties."

The members of the Convention were plainly growing tired and there are evidences of haste in the work of the last few days. There was a tendency to ride rough-shod over those whose temperaments forced them to demand modifications in petty matters. This precipitancy gave rise to considerable dissatisfaction and led several delegates to declare that they would not sign the completed document. But on the whole the sentiment of the Convention was overwhelmingly favorable. Accordingly on Saturday, the 8th of September, a new committee was appointed, to consist of five members, whose duty it was "to revise the stile of and arrange the articles which had been agreed to by the House." The committee was chosen by ballot and was made up exclusively of friends of the new Constitution: Doctor Johnson of Connecticut, Alexander Hamilton, who had returned to Philadelphia to help in finishing the work, Gouverneur Morris, James Madison, and Rufus King. On Wednesday the twelfth, the Committee made its report, the greatest credit for which is probably to be given to Morris, whose powers of expression were so greatly admired. Another day was spent in waiting for the report to be printed. But on Thursday this was ready, and three days were devoted to going over carefully each article and section and giving the finishing touches. By Saturday the work of the Convention was brought to a close, and the Constitution was then ordered to be engrossed. On Monday, the 17th of September, the Convention met for the last time. A few of those present being unwilling to sign, Gouverneur Morris again cleverly devised a form which would make the action appear to be unanimous: "Done in Convention by the unanimous consent of the states present . . . in witness whereof we have hereunto subscribed our names." Thirty-nine delegates, representing twelve States, then signed the Constitution.

When Charles Biddle of Philadelphia, who was acquainted with most of the members of the Convention, wrote his *Autobiography*, which was published in 1802, he declared that for his part he considered the government established by the Constitution to be "the best in the world, and as perfect as any human form of government can be." But he prefaced that declaration with a statement that some of the best informed members of the Federal Convention had told him "they did not believe a single member was *perfectly* satisfied with the Constitution, but they believed it was the best they could ever agree upon, and that it was infinitely better to have such a one than break up without fixing on some form of government, which I believe at one time it was expected they would have done."

One of the outstanding characteristics of the members of the Federal Convention was their practical sagacity. They had a very definite object before them. No matter how much the members might talk about democracy in theory or about ancient confederacies, when it came to action they did not go outside of their own experience. The Constitution was devised to correct well-known defects and it contained few provisions which had not been tested by practical political experience. Before the Convention met, some of the leading men in the country had prepared lists of the defects which existed in the Articles of Confederation, and in the Constitution practically every one of these defects was corrected and by means which had already been tested in the States and under the Articles of Confederation.

CHAPTER VIII

THE course of English history shows that Anglo-Saxon tradition is strongly in favor of observing precedents and of trying to maintain at least the form of law, even in revolutions. When the English people found it impossible to bear with James II and made it so uncomfortable for him that he fled the country, they shifted the responsibility from their own shoulders by charging him with "breaking the original Contract between King and People." When the Thirteen Colonies had reached the point where they felt that they must separate from England, their spokesman, Thomas Jefferson, found the necessary justification in the fundamental compact of the first settlers "in the wilds of America" where "the emigrants thought proper to adopt that system of laws under which they had hitherto lived in the mother country"; and in the Declaration of Independence he charged the King of Great Britain with "repeated injuries and usurpations all having in direct object the establishment of an absolute Tyranny over these States."

And so it was with the change to the new form of government in the United States, which was accomplished only by disregarding the forms prescribed in the Articles of Confederation and has been called, therefore, "the Revolution of 1789." From the outset the new constitution was placed under the sanction of the old. The movement began with an attempt, outwardly at least, to revise the Articles of Confederation and in that form was authorized by Congress. The first breach with the past was made when the proposal in the Virginia Resolutions was accepted that amendments made by the Convention in the Articles of Confederation should be submitted to assemblies chosen by the people instead of to the legislatures of the separate States. This was the more readily accepted because it was believed that ratification by the legislatures would result in the formation of a treaty rather than in a working instrument of government. The next step was to prevent the work of the Convention from meeting the fate of all previous amendments to the Articles of Confederation, which had required the consent of every State in

the Union.   At the time the committee of detail
made its report, the Convention was ready to agree
that the consent of all the States was not necessary,
and it eventually decided that, when ratified by the
conventions of nine States, the Constitution should
go into effect between the States so ratifying.

It was not within the province of the Convention
to determine what the course of procedure should
be in the individual States; so it simply transmitted
the Constitution to Congress and in an accompany-
ing document, which significantly omitted any request for the approval of Congress, strongly expressed the opinion that the Constitution should
"be submitted to a convention of delegates chosen
in each state by the people thereof."   This was
nothing less than indirect ratification by the people;
and, since it was impossible to foretell in advance
which of the States would or would not ratify, the
original draft of "We, the People of the States
of New Hampshire, Massachusetts, Rhode Island,
. . ." was changed to the phrase "We, the People
of the United States."   No man of that day could
imagine how significant this change would appear
in the light of later history.

Congress did not receive the new Constitution
enthusiastically, yet after a few days' discussion

it unanimously voted, eleven States being present, that the recommendations of the Convention should be followed, and accordingly sent the document to the States, but without a word of approval or disapproval. On the whole the document was well received, especially as it was favored by the upper class, who had the ability and the opportunity for expression and were in a position to make themselves heard. For a time it looked as if the Constitution would be readily adopted.

The contest over the Constitution in the States is usually taken as marking the beginning of the two great national political parties in the United States. This was, indeed, in a way the first great national question that could cause such a division. There had been, to be sure, Whigs and Tories in America, reproducing British parties, but when the trouble with the mother country began, the successive congresses of delegates were recognized and attended only by the so-called American Whigs, and after the Declaration of Independence the name of Tory became a reproach, so that with the end of the war the Tory party disappeared. After the Revolution there were local parties in the various States, divided on one and another question, such as that of hard and soft money, and these issues had coincided in different States; but they were in no sense national parties with organizations, platforms, and leaders; they were purely local, and the followers of one or the other would have denied that they were anything else than Whigs. But a new issue was now raised. The Whig party split in two, new leaders appeared, and the elements gathered in two main divisions — the Federalists advocating, and the Anti-Federalists opposing, the adoption of the new Constitution.

There were differences of opinion over all the questions which had led to the calling of the Federal Convention and the framing of the Constitution and so there was inevitably a division upon the result of the Convention's work. There were those who wanted national authority for the suppression of disorder and of what threatened to be anarchy throughout the Union; and on the other hand there were those who opposed a strongly organized government through fear of its destroying liberty. Especially debtors and creditors took opposite sides, and most of the people in the United States could have been brought under one or the other category. The former favored a system of government and legislation which would tend to relieve or postpone the payment of debts; and, as that relief would come more readily from the State Governments, they were naturally the friends of State rights and State authority and were opposed to any enlargement of the powers of the Federal Government. On the other hand, were those who felt the necessity of preserving inviolate every private and public obligation and who saw that the separate power of the States could not accomplish what was necessary to sustain both public and private credit; they were disposed to use the resources of the Union and accordingly to favor the strengthening of the national government. In nearly every State there was a struggle between these classes.

In Philadelphia and the neighborhood there was great enthusiasm for the new Constitution. Almost simultaneously with the action by Congress, and before notification of it had been received, a motion was introduced in the Pennsylvania Assembly to call a ratifying convention. The Anti-Federalists were surprised by the suddenness of this proposal and to prevent action absented themselves from the session of the Assembly, leaving that body two short of the necessary quorum for the transaction of business. The excitement and indignation in the city were so great that early the next morning a crowd gathered, dragged two of the absentees from their lodgings to the State House, and held them firmly in their places until the roll was called and a quorum counted, when the House proceeded to order a State convention. As soon as the news of this vote got out, the city gave itself up to celebrating the event by the suspension of business, the ringing of church bells, and other demonstrations. The elections were hotly contested, but the Federalists were generally successful. The convention met towards the end of November and, after three weeks of futile discussion, mainly upon trivial matters and the meaning of words, ratified the Constitution on the 12th of December, by a vote of forty-six to twenty-three. Again the city of Philadelphia celebrated.

Pennsylvania was the first State to call a convention, but its final action was anticipated by Delaware, where the State convention met and ratified the Constitution by unanimous vote on the 7th of December. The New Jersey convention spent only a week in discussion and then voted, also unanimously, for ratification on the 18th of December. The next State to ratify was Georgia, where the Constitution was approved without a dissenting vote on January 2, 1788. Connecticut followed immediately and, after a session of only five days, declared itself in favor of the Constitution, on the 9th of January, by a vote of over three to one.

The results of the campaign for ratification thus far were most gratifying to the Federalists, but the issue was not decided. With the exception of Pennsylvania, the States which had acted were of lesser importance, and, until Massachusetts, New York, and Virginia should declare themselves, the outcome would be in doubt. The convention of Massachusetts met on the same day that the Connecticut convention adjourned. The sentiment of Boston, like that of Philadelphia, was strongly Federalist; but the outlying districts, and in particular the western part of the State, where Shays' Rebellion had broken out, were to be counted in the opposition. There were 355 delegates who took part in the Massachusetts convention, a larger number than was chosen in any of the other States, and the majority seemed to be opposed to ratification. The division was close, however, and it was believed that the attitude of two men would determine the result. One of these was Governor John Hancock, who was chosen chairman of the convention but who did not attend the sessions at the outset, as he was confined to his house by an attack of gout, which, it was maliciously said, would disappear as soon as it was known which way the majority of the convention would vote. The other was Samuel Adams, a genuine friend of liberty, who was opposed on principle to the general theory of the government set forth in the Constitution. "I stumble at the threshold," he wrote. "I meet with a national government, instead of a federal union of sovereign states." But, being a shrewd politician, Adams did not commit himself openly and, when the tradesmen of Boston declared themselves in favor of ratification, he was ready to yield his personal opinion.

There were many delegates in the Massachusetts convention who felt that it was better to amend the document before them than to try another Federal Convention, when as good an instrument might not be devised. If this group were added to those who were ready to accept the Constitution as it stood, they would make a majority in favor of the new government. But the delay involved in amending was regarded as dangerous, and it was argued that, as the Constitution made ample provision for changes, it would be safer and wiser to rely upon that method. The question was one, therefore, of immediate or future amendment. Pressure was accordingly brought to bear upon Governor Hancock and intimations were made to him of future political preferment, until he was persuaded to propose immediate ratification of the Constitution, with an urgent recommendation of such amendments as would remove the objections of the Massachusetts people. When this proposal was approved by Adams, its success was assured, and a few days later, on the 6th of February, the convention voted 187 to 168 in favor of ratification. Nine amendments, largely in the nature of a bill of rights, were then demanded, and the Massachusetts representatives in Congress were enjoined "at all times, . . . to exert all their influence, and use all reasonable and legal methods, To obtain a ratification of the said alterations and provisions." On the very day this action was taken, Jefferson wrote from Paris to Madison: "I wish with all my soul that the nine first conventions may accept the new Constitution, to secure to us the good it contains; but I equally wish that the four latest, whichever they may be, may refuse to accede to it till a declaration of rights be annexed."

Boston proceeded to celebrate as Philadelphia, and Benjamin Lincoln wrote to Washington, on the 9th of February, enclosing an extract from the local paper describing the event:

By the paper your Excellency will observe some account of the parade of the Eighth the printer had by no means time enō to do justice to the subject. To give you some idea how far he has been deficient I will mention an observation I heard made by a Lady the last evening who saw the whole that the description in the paper would no more compare with the original than the light of the faintest star would with that of the Sun fortunately for us the whole ended without the least disorder and the town during the whole evening was, so far as I could observe perfectly quiet.[1]

He added another paragraph which he later struck out as being of little importance; but it throws an interesting sidelight upon the customs of the time.

The Gentlemen provided at Faneul Hall some biscuit & cheese four q᙮ Casks of wine three barrels & two hogˢ of punch the moment they found that the people had drank sufficiently means were taken to overset the two hogˢ punch this being done the company dispersed and the day ended most agreeably.[2]

Maryland came next. When the Federal Convention was breaking up, Luther Martin was speaking of the new system of government to his colleague, Daniel of St. Thomas Jenifer, and exclaimed: "I'll be hanged if ever the people of Maryland agree to it!" To which his colleague

[1] *Documentary History*, vol. iv, pp. 488–490.   [2] *Ibid.*

retorted: "I advise you to stay in Philadelphia, lest you should be hanged." And Jenifer proved to be right, for in Maryland the Federalists obtained control of the convention and, by a vote of 63 to 11, ratified the Constitution on the 26th of April.

In South Carolina, which was the Southern State next in importance to Virginia, the compromise on the slave trade proved to be one of the deciding factors in determining public opinion. When the elections were held, they resulted in an overwhelming majority for the Federalists, so that after a session of less than two weeks the convention ratified the Constitution, on the 28th of May, by a vote of over two to one.

The only apparent setback which the adoption of the Constitution had thus far received was in New Hampshire, where the convention met early in February and then adjourned until June to see what the other States might do. But this delay proved to be of no consequence for, when the time came for the second meeting of the New Hampshire delegates, eight States had already acted favorably and adoption was regarded as a certainty. This was sufficient to put a stop to any further waiting, and New Hampshire added its name to the list on the 21st of June; but the division of opinion was fairly well represented by the smallness of the majority, the vote standing 57 to 46.

Nine States had now ratified the Constitution and it was to go into effect among them. But the support of Virginia and New York was of so much importance that their decisions were awaited with uneasiness. In Virginia, in spite of the support of such men as Washington and Madison, the sentiment for and against the Constitution was fairly evenly divided, and the opposition numbered in its ranks other names of almost equal influence, such as Patrick Henry and George Mason. Feeling ran high; the contest was a bitter one and, even after the elections had been held and the convention had opened, early in June, the decision was in doubt and remained in doubt until the very end. The situation was, in one respect at least, similar to that which had existed in Massachusetts, in that it was possible to get a substantial majority in favor of the Constitution provided certain amendments were made. The same arguments were used, strengthened on the one side by what other States had done, and on the other side by the plea that now was the time to hold out for amendments. The example of Massachusetts, however, seems to have been decisive, and on the 25th of June, four days later than

New Hampshire, the Virginia convention voted to ratify, "under the conviction that whatsoever imperfections may exist in the Constitution ought rather to be examined in the mode prescribed therein, than to bring the Union into danger by delay, with a hope of obtaining amendments previous to the ratification."

When the New York convention began its sessions on the 17th of June, it is said that more than two-thirds of the delegates were Anti-Federalist in sentiment. How a majority in favor of the Constitution was obtained has never been adequately explained, but it is certain that the main credit for the achievement belongs to Alexander Hamilton. He had early realized how greatly it would help the prospects of the Constitution if thinking people could be brought to an appreciation of the importance and value of the new form of government. In order to reach the intelligent public everywhere, but particularly in New York, he projected a series of essays which should be published in the newspapers, setting forth the aims and purposes of the Constitution. He secured the assistance of Madison and Jay, and before the end of October, 1787, published the first essay in *The Independent Gazetteer*. From that time on these papers continued to be printed over the signature of "Publius," sometimes as many as three or four in a week. There were eighty-five numbers altogether, which have ever since been known as *The Federalist*. Of these approximately fifty were the work of Hamilton, Madison wrote about thirty and Jay five. Although the essays were widely copied in other journals, and form for us the most important commentary on the Constitution, making what is regarded as one of America's greatest books, it is doubtful how much immediate influence they had. Certainly in the New York convention itself Hamilton's personal influence was a stronger force. His arguments were both eloquent and cogent, and met every objection; and his efforts to win over the opposition were unremitting. The news which came by express riders from New Hampshire and then from Virginia were also deciding factors, for New York could not afford to remain out of the new Union if it was to embrace States on either side. And yet the debate continued, as the opposition was putting forth every effort to make ratification conditional upon certain amendments being adopted. But Hamilton resolutely refused to make any concessions and at length was successful in persuading the New York convention, by a vote of 30 against

27, on the 26th of July, to follow the example of Massachusetts and Virginia and to ratify the Constitution with merely a recommendation of future amendments.

The satisfaction of the country at the outcome of the long and momentous struggle over the adoption of the new government was unmistakable. Even before the action of New York had been taken, the Fourth of July was made the occasion for a great celebration throughout the United States, both as the anniversary of independence and as the consummation of the Union by the adoption of the Constitution.

The general rejoicing was somewhat tempered, however, by the reluctance of North Carolina and Rhode Island to come under "the new roof." Had the convention which met on the 21st of July in North Carolina reached a vote, it would probably have defeated the Constitution, but it was doubtless restrained by the action of New York and adjourned without coming to a decision. A second convention was called in September, 1789, and in the meantime the new government had come into operation and was bringing pressure to bear upon the recalcitrant States which refused to abandon the old union for the new. One of the earliest acts passed by Congress was a revenue act, levying duties upon foreign goods imported, which were made specifically to apply to imports from Rhode Island and North Carolina. This was sufficient for North Carolina, and on November 21, 1789, the convention ratified the Constitution. But Rhode Island still held out. A convention of that State was finally called to meet in March, 1790, but accomplished nothing and avoided a decision by adjourning until May. The Federal Government then proceeded to threaten drastic measures by taking up a bill which authorized the President to suspend all commercial intercourse with Rhode Island and to demand of that State the payment of its share of the Federal debt. The bill passed the Senate but stopped there, for the State gave in and ratified the Constitution on the 29th of May. Two weeks later Ellsworth, who was now United States Senator from Connecticut, wrote that Rhode Island had been "brought into the Union, and by a pretty cold measure in Congress, which would have exposed me to some censure, had it not produced the effect which I expected it would and which in fact it has done. But 'all is well that ends well.' The Constitution is now adopted by all the States and I have much satisfaction, and perhaps some vanity, in seeing, at length, a great work finished, for which I have long labored incessantly."[1]

Perhaps the most striking feature of these conventions is the trivial character of the objections that were raised. Some of the arguments, it is true, went to the very heart of the matter and considered the fundamental principles of government. It is possible to tolerate and even to sympathize with a man who declared:

Among other deformities the Constitution has an awful squinting. It squints toward monarchy; . . . your president may easily become a king. . . . If your American chief be a man of ambition and ability how easy it is for him to render himself absolute. We shall have a king. The army will salute him monarch.[1]

But it is hard to take seriously a delegate who asked permission "to make a short apostrophe to liberty," and then delivered himself of this bathos:

O liberty! — thou greatest good — thou fairest property — with thee I wish to live — with thee I wish to die! — Pardon me if I drop a tear on the peril to which she is exposed; I cannot, sir, see this brightest of jewels tarnished! a jewel worth ten thousand worlds! and shall we part with it so soon? O no![2]

---

[1] "Connecticut's Ratification of the Federal Constitution," by B. C. Steiner, in *Proceedings of the American Antiquarian Society*, April, 1915, pp. 88–89.

[2] Elliot's *Debates on the Federal Constitution*, vol. iii, p. 144.

There might be some reason in objecting to the excessive power vested in Congress; but what is one to think of the fear that imagined the greatest point of danger to lie in the ten miles square which later became the District of Columbia, because the Government might erect a fortified stronghold which would be invincible? Again, in the light of subsequent events it is laughable to find many protesting that, although each house was required to keep a journal of proceedings, it was only required "*from time to time* to publish the same, excepting such parts as may in their judgment require secrecy." All sorts of personal charges were made against those who were responsible for the framing of the Constitution. Hopkinson wrote to Jefferson in April, 1788:

You will be surprised when I tell you that our public News Papers have anounced General Washington to be a Fool influenced & lead by that Knave Dr. Franklin, who is a public Defaulter for Millions of Dollars, that Mr. Morris has defrauded the Public out of as many Millions as you please & that they are to cover their frauds by this new Government.[1]

All things considered, it is difficult to avoid the conclusion that such critics and detractors were trying to find excuses for their opposition.

[1] *Documentary History of the Constitution*, vol. iv, p. 563.

The majorities in the various conventions can hardly be said really to represent the people of their States, for only a small percentage of the people had voted in electing them; they were representative rather of the propertied upper class. This circumstance has given rise to the charge that the Constitution was framed and adopted by men who were interested in the protection of property, in the maintenance of the value of government securities, and in the payment of debts which had been incurred by the individual States in the course of the Revolution. Property-holders were unquestionably assisted by the mere establishment of a strong government. The creditor class seemed to require some special provision and, when the powers of Congress were under consideration in the Federal Convention, several of the members argued strongly for a positive injunction on Congress to assume obligations of the States. The chief objection to this procedure seemed to be based upon the fear of benefiting speculators rather than the legitimate creditors, and the matter was finally compromised by providing that all debts should be "as valid against the United States under this Constitution as under the Confederation." The charge that the Constitution was framed and its adoption obtained by men of property and wealth is undoubtedly true, but it is a mistake to attribute unworthy motives to them. The upper classes in the United States were generally people of wealth and so would be the natural holders of government securities. They were undoubtedly acting in self-protection, but the responsibility rested upon them to take the lead. They were acting indeed for the public interest in the largest sense, for conditions in the United States were such that every man might become a landowner and the people in general therefore wished to have property rights protected.

In the autumn of 1788 the Congress of the old Confederation made testamentary provision for its heir by voting that presidential electors should be chosen on the first Wednesday in January, 1789; that these electors should meet and cast their votes for President on the first Wednesday in February; and that the Senate and House of Representatives should assemble on the first Wednesday in March. It was also decided that the seat of government should be in the City of New York until otherwise ordered by Congress. In accordance with this procedure, the requisite elections were held, and the new government was duly installed. It happened in 1789 that the first Wednesday in March was the fourth day of that month, which thereby became the date for the beginning of each subsequent administration.

The acid test of efficiency was still to be applied to the new machinery of government. But Americans then, as now, were an adaptable people, with political genius, and they would have been able to make almost any form of government succeed. If the Federal Convention had never met, there is good reason for believing that the Articles of Confederation, with some amendments, would have been made to work. The success of the new government was therefore in a large measure dependent upon the favor of the people. If they wished to do so, they could make it win out in spite of obstacles. In other words, the new government would succeed exactly to the extent to which the people stood back of it. This was the critical moment when the slowly growing prosperity, described at length and emphasized in the previous chapters, produced one of its most important effects. In June, 1788, Washington wrote to Lafayette:

I expect, that many blessings will be attributed to our new government, which are now taking their rise from that industry and frugality into the practice of which the people have been forced from necessity. I really believe that there never was so much labour and economy to be found before in the country as at the present moment.   If they persist in the habits they are acquiring, the good effects will soon be distinguishable. When the people shall find themselves secure under an energetic government, when foreign Nations shall be disposed to give us equal advantages in commerce from dread of retaliation, when the burdens of the war shall be in a manner done away by the sale of western lands, when the seeds of happiness which are sown here shall begin to expand themselves, and when every one (under his own vine and fig-tree) shall begin to taste the fruits of freedom — then all these blessings (for all these blessings will come) will be referred to the fostering influence of the new government.   Whereas many causes will have conspired to produce them.

A few months later a similar opinion was expressed by Crèvecœur in writing to Jefferson:

Never was so great a change in the opinion of the best people as has happened these five years; almost everybody feels the necessity of coercive laws, government, union, industry, and labor. . . .   The exports of this country have singularly increased within these two years, and the imports have decreased in proportion.

The new Federal Government was fortunate in beginning its career at the moment when returning prosperity was predisposing the people to think well of it. The inauguration of Washington marked the opening of a new era for the people of the United States of America.

APPENDIX[1]

THE DECLARATION OF INDEPENDENCE — 1776

IN CONGRESS, JULY 4, 1776

The unanimous Declaration of the thirteen united States of America

WHEN in the Course of human events, it becomes necessary for one people to dissolve the political bands which have connected them with another, and to assume among the Powers of the earth, the separate and equal station to which the Laws of Nature and of Nature's God entitle them, a decent respect to the opinions of mankind requires that they should declare the causes which impel them to the separation.

We hold these truths to be self-evident, that all men are created equal, that they are endowed by their Creator with certain unalienable Rights, that among these are Life, Liberty and the pursuit of Happiness. That to secure these rights, Governments are instituted among Men, deriving their just powers from the consent of the governed, That whenever any Form of Government becomes destructive of these ends, it is the

[1] The documents in this Appendix follow the text of the *Revised Statutes of the United States*, Second Edition, 1878.

Right of the People to alter or to abolish it, and to institute new Government, laying its foundation on such principles and organizing its powers in such form, as to them shall seem most likely to effect their Safety and Happiness. Prudence, indeed, will dictate that Governments long established should not be changed for light and transient causes; and accordingly all experience hath shown, that mankind are more disposed to suffer, while evils are sufferable, than to right themselves by abolishing the forms to which they are accustomed. But when a long train of abuses and usurpations, pursuing invariably the same Object evinces a design to reduce them under absolute Despotism, it is their right, it is their duty, to throw off such Government, and to provide new Guards for their future security. — Such has been the patient sufferance of these Colonies; and such is now the necessity which constrains them to alter their former Systems of Government. The history of the present King of Great Britain is a history of repeated injuries and usurpations, all having in direct object the establishment of an absolute Tyranny over these States. To prove this, let Facts be submitted to a candid world.

He has refused his Assent to Laws, the most wholesome and necessary for the public good.

He has forbidden his Governors to pass Laws of immediate and pressing importance, unless suspended in their operation till his Assent should be obtained; and when so suspended, he has utterly neglected to attend to them.

He has refused to pass other Laws for the accommodation of large districts of people, unless those people would relinquish the right of Representation in the

Legislature, a right inestimable to them and formidable to tyrants only.

He has called together legislative bodies at places unusual, uncomfortable, and distant from the depository of their Public Records, for the sole purpose of fatiguing them into compliance with his measures.

He has dissolved Representative Houses repeatedly, for opposing with manly firmness his invasions on the rights of the people.

He has refused for a long time, after such dissolutions, to cause others to be elected; whereby the Legislative Powers, incapable of Annihilation, have returned to the People at large for their exercise; the State remaining in the mean time exposed to all the dangers of invasion from without, and convulsions within.

He has endeavoured to prevent the population of these States; for that purpose obstructing the Laws for Naturalization of Foreigners; refusing to pass others to encourage their migration hither, and raising the conditions of new Appropriations of Lands.

He has obstructed the Administration of Justice, by refusing his Assent to Laws for establishing Judiciary Powers.

He has made Judges dependent on his Will alone, for the tenure of their offices, and the amount and payment of their salaries.

He has erected a multitude of New Offices, and sent hither swarms of Officers to harrass our People, and eat out their substance.

He has kept among us, in times of peace, Standing Armies without the Consent of our legislature.

He has affected to render the Military independent of and superior to the Civil Power.

He has combined with others to subject us to a jurisdiction foreign to our constitution, and unacknowledged by our laws; giving his Assent to their acts of pretended Legislation:

For quartering large bodies of armed troops among us:

For protecting them, by a mock Trial, from Punishment for any Murders which they should commit on the Inhabitants of these States:

For cutting off our Trade with all parts of the world:

For imposing taxes on us without our Consent:

For depriving us in many cases, of the benefits of Trial by Jury:

For transporting us beyond Seas to be tried for pretended offences:

For abolishing the free System of English Laws in a neighbouring Province, establishing therein an Arbitrary government, and enlarging its Boundaries so as to render it at once an example and fit instrument for introducing the same absolute rule into these Colonies:

For taking away our Charters, abolishing our most valuable Laws, and altering fundamentally the Forms of our Government:

For suspending our own Legislature, and declaring themselves invested with Power to legislate for us in all cases whatsoever.

He has abdicated Government here, by declaring us out of his Protection and waging War against us.

He has plundered our seas, ravaged our Coasts, burnt our towns, and destroyed the lives of our people.

He is at this time transporting large armies of foreign mercenaries to compleat the works of death, desolation and tyranny, already begun with circumstances of Cruelty & perfidy scarcely paralleled in the most barbarous ages, and totally unworthy the Head of a civilized nation.

He has constrained our fellow Citizens taken Captive on the high Seas to bear Arms against their Country, to become the executioners of their friends and Brethren, or to fall themselves by their Hands.

He has excited domestic insurrections amongst us, and has endeavoured to bring on the inhabitants of our frontiers, the merciless Indian Savages, whose known rule of warfare, is an undistinguished destruction of all ages, sexes and conditions.

In every stage of these Oppressions We have Petitioned for Redress in the most humble terms: Our repeated Petitions have been answered only by repeated injury. A Prince, whose character is thus marked by every act which may define a Tyrant, is unfit to be the ruler of a free People.

Nor have We been wanting in attention to our Brittish brethren. We have warned them from time to time of attempts by their legislature to extend an unwarrantable jurisdiction over us. We have reminded them of the circumstances of our emigration and settlement here. We have appealed to their native justice and magnanimity, and we have conjured them by the ties of our common kindred to disavow these usurpations, which, would inevitably interrupt our connections and correspondence[.] They too have been deaf to the voice of justice and of consanguinity. We must, therefore, acquiesce in the necessity, which denounces our Separation, and hold them, as we hold the rest of mankind, Enemies in War, in Peace Friends.

We, therefore, the Representative of the united States of America, in General Congress, Assembled, appealing to the Supreme Judge of the world for the rectitude of our intentions, do, in the Name, and by Authority of the good People of these Colonies, solemnly publish and declare, That these United Colonies are, and of Right ought to be Free and Independent States; that they are Absolved from all Allegiance to the British Crown, and that all political connection between them and the State of Great Britain, is and ought to be totally dissolved; and that as Free and Independent States, they have full Power to levy War, conclude Peace, contract Alliances, establish Commerce, and to do all other Acts and Things which Independent States may of right do. And for the support of this Declaration, with a firm reliance on the Protection of Divine Providence, we mutually pledge to each other our Lives, our Fortunes and our sacred Honor.

JOHN HANCOCK.

New Hampshire.

JOSIAH BARTLETT,   MATTHEW THORNTON.
WM. WHIPPLE,

Massachusetts Bay.

SAML. ADAMS,   ROBT. TREAT PAINE,
JOHN ADAMS,   ELBRIDGE GERRY.

Rhode Island.

STEP. HOPKINS,   WILLIAM ELLERY.

Connecticut.

ROGER SHERMAN,   WM. WILLIAMS,
SAM'EL HUNTINGTON,   OLIVER WOLCOTT.

New York.

WM. FLOYD,
PHIL. LIVINGSTON,

FRANS. LEWIS,
LEWIS MORRIS.

New Jersey.

RICHD. STOCKTON,
JNO. WITHERSPOON,
FRAS. HOPKINSON,

JOHN HART,
ABRA. CLARK.

Pennsylvania.

ROBT. MORRIS,
BENJAMIN RUSH,
BENJA. FRANKLIN,
JOHN MORTON,
GEO. CLYMER,

JAS. SMITH,
GEO. TAYLOR,
JAMES WILSON,
GEO. ROSS.

Delaware.

CÆSAR RODNEY,
GEO. READ,

THO. M'KEAN.

Maryland.

SAMUEL CHASE,
WM. PACA,

THOS. STONE,
CHARLES CARROLL of Carrollton.

Virginia.

GEORGE WYTHE,
RICHARD HENRY LEE,
TH. JEFFERSON,
BENJA. HARRISON,

THOS. NELSON, JR.,
FRANCIS LIGHTFOOT LEE,
CARTER BRAXTON.

North Carolina.

WM. HOOPER,   JOHN PENN.
JOSEPH HEWES,

South Carolina.

EDWARD RUTLEDGE,   THOMAS LYNCH, JUNR.,
THOS. HEYWARD, JUNR.,   ARTHUR MIDDLETON.

Georgia.

BUTTON GWINNETT,   GEO. WALTON.
LYMAN HALL,

NOTE.—Mr. Ferdinand Jefferson, Keeper of the Rolls in the Department of State, at Washington, says: "The names of the signers are spelt above as in the fac-simile of the original, but the punctuation of them is not always the same; neither do the names of the States appear in the fac-simile of the original. The names of the signers of each State are grouped together in the fac-simile of the original, except the name of Matthew Thornton, which follows that of Oliver Wolcott."

ARTICLES OF CONFEDERATION — 1777.

To all to whom these Presents shall come, we the under-
signed Delegates of the States affixed to our Names
send greeting.

WHEREAS the Delegates of the United States of
America in Congress assembled did on the fifteenth
day of November in the Year of our Lord One
Thousand Seven Hundred and Seventyseven, and
in the Second Year of the Independence of America
agree to certain articles of Confederation and per-
petual Union between the States of Newhampshire,
Massachusetts-bay, Rhodeisland and Providence
Plantations, Connecticut, New York, New Jersey,
Pennsylvania, Delaware, Maryland, Virginia, North-
Carolina, South-Carolina and Georgia in the Words
following, viz.

"*Articles of Confederation and perpetual Union between*
the States of Newhampshire, Massachusetts-bay,
Rhodeisland and Providence Plantations, Con-
necticut, New-York, New-Jersey, Pennsylvania,
Delaware, Maryland, Virginia, North-Carolina,
South-Carolina and Georgia.

ARTICLE I. The stile of this confederacy shall be
"The United States of America."

ARTICLE II. Each State retains its sovereignty, freedom and independence, and every power, jurisdiction and right, which is not by this confederation expressly delegated to the United States, in Congress assembled.

ARTICLE III. The said States hereby severally enter into a firm league of friendship with each other, for their common defence, the security of their liberties, and their mutual and general welfare, binding themselves to assist each other, against all force offered to, or attacks made upon them, or any of them, on account of religion, sovereignty, trade, or any other pretence whatever.

ARTICLE IV. The better to secure and perpetuate mutual friendship and intercourse among the people of the different States in this Union, the free inhabitants of each of these States, paupers, vagabonds and fugitives from justice excepted, shall be entitled to all privileges and immunities of free citizens in the several States; and the people of each State shall have free ingress and regress to and from any other State, and shall enjoy therein all the privileges of trade and commerce, subject to the same duties, impositions and restrictions as the inhabitants thereof respectively, provided that such restrictions shall not extend so far as to prevent the removal of property imported into any State, to any other State of which the owner is an inhabitant; provided also that no imposition, duties or restriction shall be laid by any State, on the property of the United States, or either of them.

If any person guilty of, or charged with treason, felony, or other high misdemeanor in any State, shall flee from justice, and be found in any of the United States, he shall upon demand of the Governor or Executive power, of the State from which he fled, be delivered up and removed to the State having jurisdiction of his offence.

Full faith and credit shall be given in each of these States to the records, acts and judicial proceedings of the courts and magistrates of every other State.

ARTICLE V. For the more convenient management of the general interests of the United States, delegates shall be annually appointed in such manner as the legislature of each State shall direct, to meet in Congress on the first Monday in November, in every year, with a power reserved to each State, to recall its delegates, or any of them, at any time within the year, and to send others in their stead, for the remainder of the year.

No State shall be represented in Congress by less than two, nor by more than seven members; and no person shall be capable of being a delegate for more than three years in any term of six years; nor shall any person, being a delegate, be capable of holding any office under the United States, for which he, or another for his benefit receives any salary, fees or emolument of any kind.

Each State shall maintain its own delegates in a meeting of the States, and while they act as members of the committee of the States.

In determining questions in the United States, in Congress assembled, each State shall have one vote.

Freedom of speech and debate in Congress shall not be impeached or questioned in any court, or place out of Congress, and the members of Congress shall be protected in their persons from arrests and imprisonments, during the time of their going to and from, and attendance on Congress, except for treason, felony, or breach of the peace.

ARTICLE VI. No State without the consent of the United States in Congress assembled, shall send any embassy to, or receive any embassy from, or enter into any conference, agreement, alliance or treaty with any king prince or state; nor shall any person holding any office of profit or trust under the United States, or any of them, accept of any present, emolument, office or title of any kind whatever from any king, prince or foreign state; nor shall the United States in Congress assembled, or any of them, grant any title of nobility.

No two or more States shall enter into any treaty, confederation or alliance whatever between them, without the consent of the United States in Congress assembled, specifying accurately the purposes for which the same is to be entered into, and how long it shall continue.

No state shall lay any imposts or duties, which may interfere with any stipulations in treaties, entered into by the United States in Congress assembled, with any king, prince or state, in pursuance of any treaties already proposed by Congress, to the courts of France and Spain.

No vessels of war shall be kept up in time of peace by any State, except such number only, as shall be deemed necessary by the United States in Congress assembled, for the defence of such State, or its trade; nor shall any body of forces be kept up by any State, in time of peace, except such number only, as in the judgment of the United States, in Congress assembled, shall be deemed requisite to garrison the forts necessary for the defence of such State; but every State shall always keep up a well regulated and disciplined militia, sufficiently armed and accoutered, and shall provide and constantly have ready for use, in public stores, a due number of field pieces and tents, and a proper quantity of arms, ammunition and camp equipage.

No State shall engage in any war without the consent of the United States in Congress assembled, unless such State be actually invaded by enemies, or shall have received certain advice of a resolution being formed by some nation of Indians to invade such State, and the danger is so imminent as not to admit of a delay, till the United States in Congress assembled can be consulted: nor shall any State grant commissions to any ships or vessels of war, nor letters of marque or reprisal, except it be after a declaration of war by the United States in Congress assembled, and then only against the kingdom or state and the subjects thereof, against which war has been so declared, and under such regulations as shall be established by the United States in Congress assembled, unless such State be infested by pirates, in which case vessels of war may be fitted out for that occasion, and kept so long as the danger shall continue, or until the United States in Congress assembled shall determine otherwise.

ARTICLE VII.   When land-forces are raised by any State for the common defence, all officers of or under the rank of colonel, shall be appointed by the Legislature of each State respectively by whom such forces shall be raised, or in such manner as such State shall direct, and all vacancies shall be filled up by the State which first made the appointment.

ARTICLE VIII.   All charges of war, and all other expenses that shall be incurred for the common defence or general welfare, and allowed by the United States in Congress assembled, shall be defrayed out of a common treasury, which shall be supplied by the several States, in proportion to the value of all land within each State, granted to or surveyed for any person, as such land and the buildings and improvements thereon shall be estimated according to such mode as the United States in Congress assembled, shall from time to time direct and appoint.

The taxes for paying that proportion shall be laid and levied by the authority and direction of the Legislatures of the several States within the time agreed upon by the United States in Congress assembled.

Article IX. The United States in Congress assembled, shall have the sole and exclusive right and power of determining on peace and war, except in the cases mentioned in the sixth article — of sending and receiving ambassadors — entering into treaties and alliances, provided that no treaty of commerce shall be made whereby the legislative power of the respective States shall be restrained from imposing such imposts and duties on foreigners, as their own people are subjected to, or from prohibiting the exportation or importation of any species of goods or commodities whatsoever — of establishing rules for deciding in all cases, what captures on land or water shall be legal, and in what manner prizes taken by land or naval forces in the service of the United States shall be divided or appropriated — of granting letters of marque and reprisal in times of peace — appointing courts for the trial of piracies and felonies committed on the high seas and establishing courts for receiving and determining finally appeals in all cases of captures, provided that no member of Congress shall be appointed a judge of any of the said courts.

The United States in Congress assembled shall also be the last resort on appeal in all disputes and differences now subsisting or that hereafter may arise between two or more States concerning boundary, jurisdiction or any other cause whatever; which authority shall always be exercised in the manner following. Whenever the legislative or executive authority or lawful agent of any State in controversy with another shall present a petition to Congress, stating the matter in question and praying for a hearing, notice thereof shall be given by order of Congress to the legislative or executive authority of the other State in controversy, and a day assigned for the appearance of the parties by their lawful agents, who shall then be directed to appoint by joint consent, commissioners or judges to constitute a court for hearing and determining the matter in question: but if they cannot agree, Congress shall name three persons out of each of the United States, and from the list of such persons each party shall alternately strike out one, the petitioners beginning, until the number shall be reduced to thirteen; and from that number not less than seven, nor more than nine names as Congress shall direct, shall in the presence of Congress be drawn out by lot, and the persons whose names shall be so drawn or any five of them, shall be commissioners or judges, to hear and finally determine the controversy, so always as a major part of the judges who shall hear the cause shall agree in the determination: and if either party shall neglect to attend at the day appointed, without showing reasons, which Congress shall judge sufficient, or being present shall refuse to strike, the Congress shall proceed to nominate three persons out of each State, and the Secretary of Congress shall strike in behalf of such party absent or refusing; and the judgment and sentence of the court to be appointed, in the manner before prescribed, shall be final and conclusive; and if any of the parties shall refuse to submit to the authority of such court, or to appear or defend their claim or cause, the court shall nevertheless proceed to pronounce sentence, or judgment, which shall in like manner be final and decisive, the judgment or sentence and other proceedings being in either case transmitted to Congress, and lodged among the acts of Congress for the security of the parties concerned: provided that every commissioner, before he sits in judgment, shall take an oath to be administered by one of the judges of the supreme or superior court of the State where the cause shall be tried, "well and truly to hear and determine the matter in question, according to the best of his judgment, without favour, affection or hope of reward:" provided also that no State shall be deprived of territory for the benefit of the United States.

All controversies concerning the private right of soil claimed under different grants of two or more States, whose jurisdiction as they may respect such lands, and the States which passed such grants are adjusted, the said grants or either of them being at the same time claimed to have originated antecedent to such settlement of jurisdiction, shall on the petition of either party to the Congress of the United States, be finally determined as near as may be in the same manner as is before prescribed for deciding disputes respecting territorial jurisdiction between different States.

The United States in Congress assembled shall also have the sole and exclusive right and power of regulating the alloy and value of coin struck by their own authority, or by that of the respective States. — fixing the standard of weights and measures throughout the United States. — regulating the trade and managing all affairs with the Indians, not members of any of the States, provided that the legislative right of any State within its own limits be not infringed or violated — establishing and regulating post-offices from one State to another, throughout all the United States, and exacting such postage on the papers passing thro' the same as may be requisite to defray the expenses of the said office — appointing all officers of the land forces, in the service of the United States, excepting regimental officers — appointing all the officers of the naval forces, and commissioning all officers whatever in the service of the United States — making rules for the government and regulation of the said land and naval forces, and directing their operations.

The United States in Congress assembled shall have authority to appoint a committee, to sit in the recess of Congress, to be denominated "a Committee of the States," and to consist of one delegate from each State; and to appoint such other committees and civil officers as may be necessary for managing the general affairs of the United States under their direction — to appoint one of their number to preside, provided that no person be allowed to serve in the office of president more than one year in any term of three years; to ascertain the necessary sums of money to be raised for the service of the United States, and to appropriate and apply the same for defraying the public expenses — to borrow money, or emit bills on the credit of the United States, transmitting every half year to the respective States an account of the sums of money so borrowed or emitted, — to build and equip a navy — to agree upon the number of land forces, and to make requisitions from each State for its quota, in proportion to the number of white inhabitants in such State; which requisition shall be binding, and thereupon the Legislature of each State shall appoint the regimental officers, raise the men and cloath, arm and equip them in a soldier like manner, at the expense of the United States; and the officers and men so cloathed, armed and equipped shall march to the place appointed, and within the time agreed on by the United States in Congress assembled: but if the United States in Congress assembled shall, on consideration of circumstances judge proper that any State should not raise men, or should raise a smaller number than its quota, and that any other State should raise a greater number of men than the quota thereof, such extra number shall be raised, officered, cloathed, armed and equipped in the same manner as the quota of such State, unless the legislature of such State shall judge that such extra number cannot be safely spared out of the same, in which case they shall raise officer, cloath, arm and equip as many of such extra number as they judge can be safely spared. And the officers and men so cloathed, armed and equipped, shall march to the place appointed, and within the time agreed on by the United States in Congress assembled.

The United States in Congress assembled shall never engage in a war, nor grant letters of marque and reprisal in time of peace, nor enter into any treaties or alliances, nor coin money, nor regulate the value thereof, nor ascertain the sums and expenses necessary for the defence and welfare of the United States, or any of them, nor emit bills, nor borrow money on the credit of the United States, nor appropriate money, nor agree upon the number of vessels of war, to be built or purchased, or the number of land or sea forces to be raised, nor appoint a commander in chief of the army or navy, unless nine States assent to the same: nor shall a question on any other point, except for adjourning from day to day be determined, unless by the votes of a majority of the United States in Congress assembled.

The Congress of the United States shall have power to adjourn to any time within the year, and to any place within the United States, so that no period of adjournment be for a longer duration than the space of six months, and shall publish the journal of their proceedings monthly, except such parts thereof relating to treaties, alliances or military operations, as in their judgment require secresy; and the yeas and nays of the delegates of each State on any question shall be entered on the journal, when it is desired by any delegate; and the delegates of a State, or any of them, at his or their request shall be furnished with a transcript of the said journal, except such parts as are above excepted, to lay before the Legislatures of the several States.

ARTICLE X.   The committee of the States, or any nine of them, shall be authorized to execute, in the recess of Congress, such of the powers of Congress as the United States in Congress assembled, by the consent of nine States, shall from time to time think expedient to vest them with; provided that no power be delegated to the said committee, for the exercise of which, by the articles of confederation, the voice of nine States in the Congress of the United States assembled is requisite.

ARTICLE XI.   Canada acceding to this confederation, and joining in the measures of the United States, shall be admitted into, and entitled to all the advantages of this Union: but no other colony shall be admitted into the same, unless such admission be agreed to by nine States.

ARTICLE XII.   All bills of credit emitted, monies borrowed and debts contracted by, or under the authority of Congress, before the assembling of the United States, in pursuance of the present confederation, shall be deemed and considered as a charge against the United States, for payment and satisfaction whereof the said United States, and the public faith are hereby solemnly pledged.

ARTICLE XIII.   Every State shall abide by the determinations of the United States in Congress assembled, on all questions which by this confederation are submitted to them.   And the articles of this confederation shall be inviolably observed by every State, and the Union shall be perpetual; nor shall any alteration at any time hereafter be made in any of them; unless such alteration be agreed to in a Congress of the United States, and be afterwards confirmed by the Legislatures of every State.

And whereas it has pleased the Great Governor of the world to incline the hearts of the Legislatures we respectively represent in Congress, to approve of, and to authorize us to ratify the said articles of confederation and perpetual union.   Know ye that we the undersigned delegates, by virtue of the power and authority to us given for that purpose, do by these presents, in the name and in behalf of our respective constituents, fully and entirely ratify and confirm each and every of the said articles of confederation and perpetual union, and all and singular the matters and things therein contained: and we do further solemnly plight and engage the faith of our respective constituents, that they shall abide by the determinations of the United States in Congress assembled, on all questions, which by the said confederation are submitted to them. And that the articles thereof shall be inviolably observed by the States we re[s]pectively represent, and that the Union shall be perpetual.

In witness whereof we have hereunto set our hands in Congress. Done at Philadelphia in the State of Pennsylvania the ninth day of July in the year of our Lord one thousand seven hundred and seventy-eight, and in the third year of the independence of America.[1]

On the part & behalf of the State of New Hampshire.

JOSIAH BARTLETT, JOHN WENTWORTH, JUNR., August 8th, 1778.

On the part and behalf of the State of Massachusetts Bay.

JOHN HANCOCK, FRANCIS DANA,
SAMUEL ADAMS, JAMES LOVELL,
ELDBRIDGE GERRY, SAMUEL HOLTEN.

[1] From the circumstances of delegates from the same State having signed the Articles of Confederation at different times, as appears by the dates, it is probable they affixed their names as they happened to be present in Congress, after they had been authorized by their constituents.

On the part and behalf of the State of Rhode Island and Providence Plantations.

WILLIAMS ELLERY,   JOHN COLLINS.
HENRY MARCHANT,

On the part and behalf of the State of Connecticut.

ROGER SHERMAN,   TITUS HOSMER,
SAMUEL HUNTINGTON,   ANDREW ADAMS.
OLIVER WOLCOTT,

On the part and behalf of the State of New York.

JAS. DUANE,   WM. DUER,
FRA. LEWIS,   GOUV. MORRIS.

On the part and in behalf of the State of New Jersey, Novr. 26, 1778.

JNO. WITHERSPOON,   NATHL. SCUDDER.

On the part and behalf of the State of Pennsylvania.

ROBT. MORRIS,   WILLIAM CLINGAN,
DANIEL ROBERDEAU,   JOSEPH REED, 22d July,
JONA. BAYARD SMITH,   1778.

On the part & behalf of the State of Delaware.

THO. M'KEAN, Feby. 12,   NICHOLAS VAN DYKE.
  1779.
JOHN DICKINSON, May 5,
  1779.

On the part and behalf of the State of Maryland.

JOHN HANSON, March 1,   DANIEL CARROLL, Mar. 1,
  1781.   1781.

On the part and behalf of the State of Virginia.

RICHARD HENRY LEE,   JNO. HARVIE,
JOHN BANISTER,   FRANCIS LIGHTFOOT LEE.
THOMAS ADAMS,

On the part and behalf of the State of No. Carolina.

JOHN PENN, July 21st,   JNO. WILLIAMS.
    1778.
CORNS. HARNETT,

On the part & behalf of the State of South Carolina.

HENRY LAURENS,   RICHD. HUTSON,
WILLIAM HENRY DRAY-   THOS. HEYWARD, JUNR.
    TON,
JNO. MATHEWS,

On the part & behalf of the State of Georgia.

JNO. WALTON, 24th July,   EDWD. LANGWORTHY.
    1778.
EDWD. TELFAIR,

THE NORTHWEST TERRITORIAL GOVERNMENT — 1787.

The Confederate Congress, July 13, 1787.

An Ordinance for the government of the territory of the United States northwest of the river Ohio.

Section 1. *Be it ordained by the United States in Congress assembled,* That the said territory, for the purpose of temporary government, be one district, subject, however, to be divided into two districts, as future circumstances may, in the opinion of Congress, make it expedient.

Sec. 2. *Be it ordained by the authority aforesaid,* That the estates both of resident and non-resident proprietors in the said territory, dying intestate, shall descend to, and be distributed among, their children and the descendants of a deceased child in equal parts, the descendants of a deceased child or grandchild to take the share of their deceased parent in equal parts among them; and where there shall be no children or descendants, then in equal parts to the next of kin, in equal degree; and among collaterals, the children of a deceased brother or sister of the intestate shall have, in equal parts among them, their deceased parent's share; and there shall, in no case, be a distinction between kindred of the whole and half blood; saving in all cases to the widow of the intestate, her third part of the real estate for life, and one-third part of the personal estate; and this law relative to descents and dower, shall remain in full force until altered by the legislature of the district. And until the governor and judges shall adopt laws as hereinafter mentioned, estates in the said territory may be devised or bequeathed by wills in writing, signed and sealed by him or her in whom the estate may be, (being of full age,) and attested by three witnesses; and real estates may be conveyed by lease and release, or bargain and sale, signed, sealed, and delivered by the person, being of full age, in whom the estate may be, and attested by two witnesses, provided such wills be duly proved, and such conveyances be acknowledged, or the execution thereof duly proved, and be recorded within one year after proper magistrates, courts, and registers, shall be appointed for that purpose; and personal property may be transferred by delivery, saving, however, to the French and Canadian inhabitants, and other settlers of the Kaskaskias, Saint Vincents, and the neighboring villages, who have heretofore professed themselves citizens of Virginia, their laws and customs now being in force among them, relative to the descent and conveyance of property.

SEC. 3. *Be it ordained by the authority aforesaid,* That there shall be appointed, from time to time, by Congress, a governor, whose commission shall continue in force for the term of three years, unless sooner revoked by Congress; he shall reside in the district, and have a freehold estate therein, in one thousand acres of land, while in the exercise of his office.

SEC. 4. There shall be appointed from time to time,

by Congress, a secretary, whose commission shall continue in force for four years, unless sooner revoked; he shall reside in the district, and have a freehold estate therein, in five hundred acres of land, while in the exercise of his office.   It shall be his duty to keep and preserve the acts and laws passed by the legislature, and the public records of the district, and the proceedings of the governor in his executive department, and transmit authentic copies of such acts and proceedings every six months to the Secretary of Congress.   There shall also be appointed a court, to consist of three judges, any two of whom to form a court, who shall have a common-law jurisdiction, and reside in the district, and have each therein a freehold estate, in five hundred acres of land, while in the exercise of their offices; and their commissions shall continue in force during good behavior.

SEC. 5.   The governor and judges, or a majority of them, shall adopt and publish in the distric[t] such laws of the original States, criminal and civil, as may be necessary, and best suited to the circumstances of the district, and report them to Congress from time to time, which laws shall be in force in the district until the organization of the general assembly therein, unless disapproved of by Congress; but afterwards the legislature shall have authority to alter them as they shall think fit.

SEC. 6.   The governor, for the time being, shall be commander-in-chief of the militia, appoint and commission all officers in the same below the rank of general officers; all general officers shall be appointed and commissioned by Congress.

SEC. 7.   Previous to the organization of the general

assembly the governor shall appoint such magistrates, and other civil officers, in each county or township, as he shall find necessary for the preservation of the peace and good order in the same. After the general assembly shall be organized the powers and duties of magistrates and other civil officers shall be regulated and defined by the said assembly; but all magistrates and other civil officers, not herein otherwise directed, shall, during the continuance of this temporary government, be appointed by the governor.

SEC. 8. For the prevention of crimes and injuries, the laws to be adopted or made shall have force in all parts of the district, and for the execution of process, criminal and civil, the governor shall make proper divisions thereof; and he shall proceed, from time to time, as circumstances may require, to lay out the parts of the district in which the Indian titles shall have been extinguished, into counties and townships, subject, however, to such alterations as may thereafter be made by the legislature.

SEC. 9. So soon as there shall be five thousand free male inhabitants, of full age, in the district, upon giving proof thereof to the governor, they shall receive authority, with time and place, to elect representatives from their counties or townships, to represent them in the general assembly: *Provided*, That for every five hundred free male inhabitants there shall be one representative, and so on, progressively, with the number of free male inhabitants, shall the right of representation increase, until the number of representatives shall amount to twenty-five; after which the number and proportion of representatives shall be regulated by the legislature: *Provided*, That no person be eligible or qualified to act as a representative, unless he shall have been a citizen of one of the United States three years, and be a resident in the district, or unless he shall have resided in the district three years; and, in either case, shall likewise hold in his own right, in fee-simple, two hundred acres of land within the same: *Provided also*, That a freehold in fifty acres of land in the district, having been a citizen of one of the States, and being resident in the district, or the like freehold and two years' residence in the district, shall be necessary to qualify a man as an elector of a representative.

SEC. 10. The representatives thus elected shall serve for the term of two years; and in case of the death of a representative, or removal from office, the governor shall issue a writ to the county or township, for which he was a member, to elect another in his stead, to serve for the residue of the term.

SEC. 11. The general assembly, or legislature, shall consist of the governor, legislative council, and a house of representatives. The legislative council shall consist of five members, to continue in office five years, unless sooner removed by Congress; any three of whom to be a quorum; and the members of the council shall be nominated and appointed in the following manner, to wit: As soon as representatives shall be elected the governor shall appoint a time and place for them to meet together, and when met they shall nominate ten persons, resident in the district, and each possessed of a freehold in five hundred acres of land, and return their names to Congress, five of whom Congress shall appoint and commission to serve as aforesaid; and whenever a vacancy shall happen in the council, by death or removal from office, the house of representatives shall nominate two persons, qualified as aforesaid, for each vacancy, and return their names to Congress, one of whom Congress shall appoint and commission for the residue of the term; and every five years, four months at least before the expiration of the time of service of the members of the council, the said house shall nominate ten persons, qualified as aforesaid, and return their names to Congress, five of whom Congress shall appoint and commission to serve as members of the council five years, unless sooner removed. And the governor, legislative council, and house of representatives shall have authority to make laws in all cases for the good government of the district, not repugnant to the principles and articles in this ordinance established and declared. And all bills, having passed by a majority in the house, and by a majority in the council, shall be referred to the governor for his assent; but no bill, or legislative act whatever, shall be of any force without his assent. The governor shall have power to convene, prorogue, and dissolve the general assembly when, in his opinion, it shall be expedient.

SEC. 12. The governor, judges, legislative council, secretary, and such other officers as Congress shall appoint in the district, shall take an oath or affirmation of fidelity, and of office; the governor before the President of Congress, and all other officers before the governor. As soon as a legislature shall be formed in the district, the council and house assembled, in one room, shall have authority, by joint ballot, to elect a delegate to Congress, who shall have a seat in Congress, with a right of debating, but not of voting, during this temporary government.

SEC. 13. And for extending the fundamental principles of civil and religious liberty, which form the basis whereon these republics, their laws and constitutions, are erected; to fix and establish those principles as the basis of all laws, constitutions, and governments, which forever hereafter shall be formed in the said territory; to provide, also, for the establishment of States, and permanent government therein, and for their admission to a share in the Federal councils on an equal footing with the original States, at as early periods as may be consistent with the general interest:

SEC. 14. It is hereby ordained and declared, by the authority aforesaid, that the following articles shall be considered as articles of compact, between the original States and the people and States in the said territory, and forever remain unalterable, unless by common consent, to wit:

ARTICLE I.

No person, demeaning himself in a peaceable and orderly manner, shall ever be molested on account of his mode of worship, or religious sentiments, in the said territories.

ARTICLE II.

The inhabitants of the said territory shall always be entitled to the benefits of the writs of *habeas corpus,* and of the trial by jury; of a propo[r]tionate representation of the people in the legislature, and of judicial proceedings according to the course of the common law. All persons shall be bailable, unless for capital offences, where the proof shall be evident, or the presumption great. All fines shall be moderate; and no cruel or unusual punishments shall be inflicted. No man shall be deprived of his liberty or property, but by the judgment of his peers, or the law of the land, and should the public exigencies make it necessary, for the common preservation, to take any person's property, or to demand his particular services, full compensation shall be made for the same. And, in the just preservation of rights and property, it is understood and declared, that no law ought ever to be made or have force in the said territory, that shall, in any manner whatever, interfere with or affect private contracts, or engagements, *bona fide*, and without fraud previously formed.

ARTICLE III.

Religion, morality, and knowledge being necessary to good government and the happiness of mankind, schools and the means of education shall forever be encouraged. The utmost good faith shall always be observed towards the Indians; their lands and property shall never be taken from them without their consent; and in their property, rights, and liberty they never shall be invaded or disturbed, unless in just and lawful wars authorized by Congress; but laws founded in justice and humanity shall, from time to time, be made, for preventing wrongs being done to them, and for preserving peace and friendship with them.

ARTICLE IV.

The said territory, and the States which may be formed therein, shall forever remain a part of this confederacy of the United States of America, subject to the Articles of Confederation, and to such alterations therein as shall be constitutionally made; and to all the acts and ordinances of the United States in Congress assembled, conformable thereto. The inhabitants and settlers in the said territory shall be subject to pay a part of the Federal debts, contracted, or to be contracted, and a proportional part of the expenses of government to be apportioned on them by Congress, according to the same common rule and measure by which apportionments thereof shall be made on the other States; and the taxes for paying their proportion shall be laid and levied by the authority and direction of the legislatures of the district, or districts, or new States, as in the original States, within the time agreed upon by the United States in Congress assembled. The legislatures of those districts, or new States, shall never interfere with the primary disposal of the soil by the United States in Congress assembled, nor with any regulations Congress may find necessary for securing the title in such soil to the *bona-fide* purchasers. No tax shall be imposed on lands the property of the United States; and in no case shall non-resident proprietors be taxed higher than residents. The navigable waters leading into the Mississippi and Saint Lawrence, and the carrying places between the same, shall be common highways, and forever free, as well to the inhabitants of the said territory as to the citizens of the United States, and those of any other States that may be admitted into the confederacy, without any tax, impost, or duty therefor.

ARTICLE V.

There shall be formed in the said territory not less than three nor more than five States; and the boundaries of the States, as soon as Virginia shall alter her act of cession and consent to the same, shall become fixed and established as follows, to wit: The western State, in the said territory, shall be bounded by the Mississippi, the Ohio, and the Wabash Rivers; a direct line drawn from the Wabash and Post Vincents, due north, to the territorial line between the United States and Canada; and by the said territorial line to the Lake of the Woods and Mississippi. The middle State shall be bounded by the said direct line, the Wabash from Post Vincents to the Ohio, by the Ohio, by a direct line drawn due north from the mouth of the Great Miami to the said territorial line, and by the said territorial line. The eastern State shall be bounded by the last-mentioned direct line, the Ohio, Pennsylvania, and the said territorial line: *Provided, however,* And it is further understood and declared, that the boundaries of these three States shall be subject so far to be altered, that, if Congress shall hereafter find it expedient, they shall have authority to form one or two States in that part of the said territory which lies north of an east and west line drawn through the southerly bend or extreme of Lake Michigan. And whenever any of the said States shall have sixty thousand free inhabitants therein, such State shall be admitted, by its delegates, into the Congress of the United States, on an equal footing with the original States, in all respects whatever; and shall be at liberty to form a permanent constitution and State government: *Provided,* The constitution and government, so to be formed, shall be republican, and in conformity to the principles contained in these articles, and, so far as it can be consistent with the general interest of the confederacy, such admission shall be allowed at an earlier period, and when there may be a less number of free inhabitants in the State than sixty thousand.

ARTICLE VI.

There shall be neither slavery nor involuntary servitude in the said territory, otherwise than in the punishment of crimes, whereof the party shall have been duly convicted: *Provided always*, That any person escaping into the same, from whom labor or service is lawfully claimed in any one of the original States, such fugitive may be lawfully reclaimed, and conveyed to the person claiming his or her labor or service as aforesaid.

Be it ordained by the authority aforesaid, That the resolutions of the 23d of April, 1784, relative to the subject of this ordinance, be, and the same are hereby, repealed, and declared null and void.

Done by the United States, in Congress assembled, the 13th day of July, in the year of our Lord 1787, and of their sovereignty and independence the twelfth.

CONSTITUTION OF THE UNITED STATES —
1787.

We THE PEOPLE of the United States, in Order to form
a more perfect Union, establish Justice, insure domestic Tranquility, provide for the common defence, promote the general Welfare, and secure the
Blessings of Liberty to ourselves and our Posterity, do ordain and establish this CONSTITUTION for
the United States of America.

ARTICLE I.

SECTION. 1. All legislative Powers herein grant-
ed shall be vested in a Congress of the United
States, which shall consist of a Senate and House of
Representatives.

SECTION. 2. [1] The House of Representatives shall
be composed of Members chosen every second Year
by the People of the several States, and the Electors
in each State shall have the Qualifications requisite
for Electors of the most numerous Branch of the
State Legislature.

[2] No Person shall be a Representative who shall not
have attained to the Age of twenty-five Years, and
been seven Years a Citizen of the United States, and
who shall not, when elected, be an Inhabitant of that
State in which he shall be chosen.

3 [Representatives and direct Taxes shall be apportioned among the several States which may be included within this Union, according to their respective Numbers, which shall be determined by adding to the whole Number of free Persons, including those bound to Service for a Term of Years, and excluding Indians not taxed, three fifths of all other Persons.] The actual Enumeration shall be made within three Years after the first Meeting of the Congress of the United States, and within every subsequent Term of ten Years, in such Manner as they shall by Law direct. The Number of Representatives shall not exceed one for every thirty Thousand, but each State shall have at Least one Representative; and until such enumeration shall be made, the State of New Hampshire shall be entitled to chuse three, Massachusetts eight, Rhode-Island and Providence Plantations one, Connecticut five, New-York six, New Jersey four, Pennsylvania eight, Delaware one, Maryland six, Virginia ten, North Carolina five, South Carolina five, and Georgia three.

4 When vacancies happen in the Representation from any State, the Executive Authority thereof shall issue Writs of Election to fill such Vacancies.

5 The House of Representatives shall chuse their Speaker and other Officers; and shall have the sole Power of Impeachment.

SECTION. 3. 1 The Senate of the United States shall be composed of two Senators from each State, chosen by the Legislature thereof, for six Years; and each Senator shall have one Vote.

2 Immediately after they shall be assembled in Consequence of the first Election, they shall be divided as equally as may be into three Classes. The Seats of the

Senators of the first Class shall be vacated at the Expiration of the second year, of the second Class at the Expiration of the fourth Year, and of the third Class at the Expiration of the sixth Year, so that one-third may be chosen every second Year; and if Vacancies happen by Resignation, or otherwise, during the Recess of the Legislature of any State, the Executive thereof may make temporary Appointments until the next Meeting of the Legislature, which shall then fill such Vacancies.

³ No Person shall be a Senator who shall not have attained to the Age of thi[r]ty Years, and been nine Years a Citizen of the United States, and who shall not, when elected, be an Inhabitant of that State for which he shall be chosen.

⁴ The Vice President of the United States shall be President of the Senate, but shall have no Vote, unless they be equally divided.

⁵ The Senate shall chuse their other Officers, and also a President pro tempore, in the Absence of the Vice President, or when he shall exercise the Office of President of the United States.

⁶ The Senate shall have the sole Power to try all Impeachments. When sitting for that Purpose, they shall be on Oath or Affirmation. When the President of the United States is tried, the Chief Justice shall preside: And no Person shall be convicted without the Concurrence of two thirds of the Members present.

⁷ Judgment in Cases of Impeachment shall not extend further than to removal from Office, and disqualification to hold and enjoy any Office of honor, Trust or Profit under the United States: but the Party convicted shall nevertheless be liable and subject to

Indictment, Trial, Judgment and Punishment, according to Law.

Section. 4. [1] The Times, Places and Manner of holding Elections for Senators and Representatives, shall be prescribed in each State by the Legislature thereof; but the Congress may at any time by Law make or alter such Regulations, except as to the Places of chusing Senators.

[2] The Congress shall assemble at least once in every Year, and such Meeting shall be on the first Monday in December, unless they shall by Law appoint a different Day.

Section. 5. [1] Each House shall be the Judge of the Elections, Returns and Qualifications of its own Members, and a Majority of each shall constitute a Quorum to do Business; but a smaller Number may adjourn from day to day, and may be authorized to compel the Attendance of absent Members, in such Manner, and under such Penalties as each House may provide.

[2] Each House may determine the Rules of its Proceedings, punish its Members for disorderly Behavior, and, with the Concurrence of two thirds, expel a Member.

[3] Each House shall keep a Journal of its Proceedings, and from time to time publish the same, excepting such Parts as may in their Judgment require Secrecy; and the Yeas and Nays of the Members of either House on any question shall, at the Desire of one fifth of those present, be entered on the Journal.

[4] Neither House, during the Session of Congress, shall, without the Consent of the other, adjourn for more than three days, nor to any other Place than that in which the two Houses shall be sitting.

SECTION. 6. [1] The Senators and Representatives shall receive a Compensation for their Services, to be ascertained by Law, and paid out of the Treasury of the United States. They shall in all Cases, except Treason, Felony and Breach of the Peace, be privileged from Arrest during their Attendance at the Session of their respective Houses, and in going to and returning from the same; and for any Speech or Debate in either House, they shall not be questioned in any other Place.

[2] No Senator or Representative shall, during the Time for which he was elected, be appointed to any civil Office under the Authority of the United States, which shall have been created, or the Emoluments whereof shall have been encreased during such time; and no Person holding any Office under the United States, shall be a Member of either House during his Continuance in Office.

SECTION. 7. [1] All Bills for raising Revenue shall originate in the House of Representatives; but the Senate may propose or concur with Amendments as on other Bills.

[2] Every Bill which shall have passed the House of Representatives and the Senate, shall, before it become a Law, be presented to the President of the United States; If he approve he shall sign it, but if not he shall return it, with his Objections to that House in which it shall have originated, who shall enter the Objections at large on their Journal, and proceed to reconsider it. If after such Reconsideration two thirds of that House shall agree to pass the Bill, it shall be sent, together with the Objections, to the other House, by which it shall likewise be reconsidered, and if approved by two thirds of that House, it shall become a

Law. But in all such Cases the Votes of both Houses shall be determined by Yeas and Nays, and the Names of the Persons voting for and against the Bill shall be entered on the Journal of each House respectively. If any Bill shall not be returned by the President within ten Days (Sundays excepted) after it shall have been presented to him, the Same shall be a Law, in like Manner as if he had signed it, unless the Congress by their Adjournment prevent its Return, in which Case it shall not be a Law.

3 Every Order, Resolution, or Vote to which the Concurrence of the Senate and House of Representatives may be necessary (except on a question of Adjournment) shall be presented to the President of the United States; and before the Same shall take Effect, shall be approved by him, or being disapproved by him, shall be repassed by two thirds of the Senate and House of Representatives, according to the Rules and Limitations prescribed in the Case of a Bill.

SECTION. 8. 1 The Congress shall have Power To lay and collect Taxes, Duties, Imposts and Excises, to pay the Debts and provide for the common Defence and general Welfare of the United States; but all Duties, Imposts and Excises shall be uniform throughout the United States;

2 To borrow Money on the credit of the United States;

3 To regulate Commerce with foreign Nations, and among the several States, and with the Indian Tribes;

4 To establish an uniform Rule of Naturalization, and uniform Laws on the subject of Bankruptcies throughout the United States;

5 To coin Money, regulate the Value thereof, and of

foreign Coin, and fix the Standard of Weights and Measures;

6 To provide for the Punishment of counterfeiting the Securities and current Coin of the United States;

7 To establish Post Offices and post Roads;

8 To promote the Progress of Science and useful Arts, by securing for limited Times to Authors and Inventors the exclusive Right to their respective Writings and Discoveries;

9 To constitute Tribunals inferior to the supreme Court;

10 To define and punish Piracies and Felonies committed on the high Seas, and Offences against the Law of Nations;

11 To declare War, grant Letters of Marque and Reprisal, and make Rules concerning Captures on Land and Water;

12 To raise and support Armies, but no Appropriation of Money to that Use shall be for a longer Term than two Years;

13 To provide and maintain a Navy;

14 To make Rules for the Government and Regulation of the land and naval Forces;

15 To provide for calling forth the Militia to execute the Laws of the Union, suppress Insurrections and repel Invasions;

16 To provide for organizing, arming, and disciplining, the Militia, and for governing such Part of them as may be employed in the Service of the United States, reserving to the States respectively, the Appointment of the Officers, and the Authority of training the Militia according to the discipline prescribed by Congress;

17 To exercise exclusive Legislation in all Cases

whatsoever, over such District (not exceeding ten Miles square) as may, by Cession of particular States, and the Acceptance of Congress, become the Seat of the Government of the United States, and to exercise like Authority over all places purchased by the Consent of the Legislature of the State in which the Same shall be, for the Erection of Forts, Magazines, Arsenals, dock-Yards, and other needful Buildings; — And

[18] To make all Laws which shall be necessary and proper for carrying into Execution the foregoing Powers, and all other Powers vested by this Constitution in the Government of the United States, or in any Department or Officer thereof.

SECTION. 9. [1] The Migration or Importation of such Persons as any of the States now existing shall think proper to admit, shall not be prohibited by the Congress prior to the Year one thousand eight hundred and eight, but a Tax or duty may be imposed on such Importation, not exceeding ten dollars for each person.

[2] The Privilege of the Writ of Habeas Corpus shall not be suspended, unless when in Cases of Rebellion or Invasion the public Safety may require it.

[3] No Bill of Attainder or expost facto Law shall be passed.

[4] No Capitation, or other direct, tax shall be laid, unless in Proportion to the Census or Enumeration herein before directed to be taken.

[5] No Tax or Duty shall be laid on Articles exported from any State.

[6] No Preference shall be given by any Regulation of Commerce or Revenue to the Ports of one State over

those of another: nor shall Vessels bound to, or from, one State, be obliged to enter, clear, or pay Duties in another.

7 No Money shall be drawn from the Treasury, but in Consequence of Appropriations made by Law; and a regular Statement and Account of the Receipts and Expenditures of all public Money shall be published from time to time.

8 No Title of Nobility shall be granted by the United States: And no Person holding any Office of Profit or Trust under them, shall, without the Consent of the Congress, accept of any present, Emolument, Office, or Title, of any kind whatever, from any King, Prince, or foreign State.

SECTION. 10. 1 No State shall enter into any Treaty, Alliance, or Confederation; grant Letters of Marque or Reprisal; coin Money; emit Bills of Credit; make any Thing but gold and silver Coin a Tender in Payment of Debts; pass any Bill of Attainder, ex post facto Law, or Law impairing the Obligation of Contracts, or grant any Title of Nobility.

2 No State shall, without the Consent of the Congress, lay any Imposts or Duties on imports or Exports, except what may be absolutely necessary for executing it's inspection Laws: and the net Produce of all Duties and Imposts, laid by any State on Imports or Exports, shall be for the Use of the Treasury of the United States; and all such Laws shall be subject to the Revision and Controul of the Congress.

3 No State shall, without the Consent of Congress, lay any Duty of Tonnage, keep Troops, or Ships of War in time of Peace, enter into any Agreement or Compact with another State, or with a foreign Power,

or engage in War, unless actually invaded, or in such imminent Danger as will not admit of delay.

ARTICLE II.

SECTION. 1.   [1] The executive Power shall be vested in a President of the United States of America.   He shall hold his Office during the Term of four Years, and, together with the Vice President, chosen for the same Term, be elected, as follows

[2] Each State shall appoint, in such Manner as the Legislature thereof may direct, a Number of Electors, equal to the whole Number of Senators and Representatives to which the State may be entitled in the Congress: but no Senator or Representative, or Person holding an Office of Trust or Profit under the United States, shall be appointed an Elector.

[3] The Congress may determine the Time of chusing the Electors, and the Day on which they shall give their Votes; which Day shall be the same throughout the United States.

[4] No Person except a natural born Citizen, or a Citizen of the United States, at the time of the Adoption of this Constitution, shall be eligible to the Office of President; neither shall any Person be eligible to that Office who shall not have attained to the Age of thirty five Years, and been fourteen Years a Resident within the United States.

[5] In Case of the Removal of the President from Office, or of his Death, Resignation, or Inability to discharge the Powers and Duties of the said Office, the same shall devolve on the Vice President, and the Congress may by Law provide for the Case of Removal,

Death, Resignation, or Inability, both of the President and Vice President, declaring what Officer shall then act as President, and such Officer shall act accordingly, until the Disability be removed, or a President shall be elected.

⁶ The President shall, at stated Times, receive for his Services, a Compensation, which shall neither be encreased nor dimished during the Period for which he shall have been elected, and he shall not receive within that Period any other Emolument from the United States, or any of them.

⁷ Before he enter on the Execution of his Office, he shall take the following Oath or Affirmation: — "I do solemnly swear (or affirm) that I will faithfully execute the Office of the President of the United States, and will to the best of my ability, preserve, protect and defend the Constitution of the United States."

SECTION. 2. ¹ The President shall be Commander in Chief of the Army and Navy of the United States, and of the Militia of the several States, when called into the actual Service of the United States; he may require the Opinion, in writing, of the principal Officer in each of the executive Departments, upon any Subject relating to the Duties of their respective Offices, and he shall have Power to grant Reprieves and Pardons for Offences against the United States, except in Cases of Impeachment.

² He shall have Power, by and with the Advice and Consent of the Senate, to make Treaties, provided two thirds of the Senators present concur; and he shall nominate, and by and with the Advice and Consent of the Senate, shall appoint Ambassadors, other public Ministers and Consuls, Judges of the supreme Court,

and all other Officers of the United States, whose Appointments are not herein otherwise provided for, and which shall be established by Law: but the Congress may by Law vest the Appointment of such inferior Officers, as they think proper, in the President alone, in the Courts of Law, or in the Heads of Departments.

³ The President shall have Power to fill up all Vacancies that may happen during the Recess of the Senate, by granting Commissions which shall expire at the End of their next Session.

SECTION. 3. He shall from time to time give to the Congress Information of the State of the Union, and recommend to their Consideration such Measures as he shall judge necessary and expedient; he may, on extraordinary Occasions, convene both Houses, or either of them, and in Case of Disagreement between them, with Respect to the Time of Adjournment, he may adjourn them to such Time as he shall think proper; he shall receive Ambassadors and other public Ministers; he shall take Care that the Laws be faithfully executed, and shall Commission all the Officers of the United States.

SECTION. 4. The President, Vice President and all civil Officers of the United States, shall be removed from Office on Impeachment for, and Conviction of, Treason, Bribery, or other high Crimes and Misdemeanors.

ARTICLE III.

SECTION. 1. The judicial Power of the United States, shall be vested in one supreme Court, and in such inferior Courts as the Congress may from time to time ordain and establish. The Judges, both of the supreme and inferior Courts, shall hold their Offices during good Behaviour, and shall, at stated Times, receive for their Services, a Compensation, which shall not be diminished during their Continuance in Office.

SECTION. 2. [1] The judicial Power shall extend to all Cases, in Law and Equity, arising under this Constitution, the Laws of the United States, and Treaties made, or which shall be made, under their Authority; — to all Cases affecting Ambassadors, other public Ministers and Consuls; — to all Cases of admiralty and maritime Jurisdiction; — to Controversies to which the United States shall be a Party; — to Controversies between two or more States; — between a State and Citizens of another State — between Citizens of different States, — between Citizens of the same State claiming Lands under Grants of different States, and between a State, or the Citizens thereof, and foreign States, Citizens or Subjects;

[2] In all Cases affecting Ambassadors, other public Ministers and Consuls, and those in which a State shall be Party, the supreme Court shall have original Jurisdiction. In all the other Cases before mentioned, the supreme Court shall have appellate Jurisdiction, both as to Law and Fact, with such Exceptions, and under such Regulations as the Congress shall make.

[3] The Trial of all Crimes, except in Cases of Impeachment, shall be by Jury; and such Trial shall be held in the State where the said Crimes shall have been committed; but when not committed within any State, the Trial shall be at such Place or Places as the Congress may by Law have directed.

SECTION. 3. [1] Treason against the United States,

shall consist only in levying War against them, or in adhering to their Enemies, giving them Aid and Comfort. No Person shall be convicted of Treason unless on the Testimony of two Witnesses to the same overt Act, or on Confession in open Court.

[2] The Congress shall have Power to declare the Punishment of Treason, but no Attainder of Treason shall work Corruption of Blood, or Forfeiture except during the Life of the Person attainted.

ARTICLE IV.

Section. 1. Full Faith and Credit shall be given in each State to the public Acts, Records, and judicial Proceedings of every other State. And the Congress may by general Laws prescribe the Manner in which such Acts, Records and Proceedings shall be proved, and the Effect thereof.

Section. 2. [1] The Citizens of each State shall be entitled to all Privileges and Immunities of Citizens in the several States.

[2] A person charged in any State with Treason, Felony, or other Crime, who shall flee from Justice, and be found in another State, shall on Demand of the Executive Authority of the State from which he fled, be delivered up to be removed to the State having jurisdiction of the Crime.

[3] No Person held to Service or Labour in one State, under the Laws thereof, escaping into another, shall, in Consequence of any Law or Regulation therein, be discharged from such Service or Labour, but shall be delivered up on Claim of the Party to whom such Service or Labour may be due.

Section. 3.   [1] New States may be admitted by the Congress into this Union; but no new State shall be formed or erected within the Jurisdiction of any other State; nor any State be formed by the Junction of two or more States, or Parts of States, without the Consent of the Legislature of the States concerned as well as of the Congress.

[2] The Congress shall have Power to dispose of and make all needful Rules and Regulations respecting the Territory or other Property belonging to the United States; and nothing in this Constitution shall be so construed as to Prejudice any Claims of the United States, or of any particular State.

Section 4.   The United States shall guarantee to every State in this Union a Republican Form of Government, and shall protect each of them against Invasion; and on Application of the Legislature, or of the Executive (when the Legislature cannot be convened) against domestic Violence.

ARTICLE V.

The Congress, whenever two thirds of both Houses shall deem it necessary, shall propose Amendments to this Constitution, or, on the Application of the Legislatures of two thirds of the several States, shall call a Convention for proposing Amendments, which, in either Case, shall be valid to all Intents and Purposes, as Part of this Constitution, when ratified by the Legislatures of three fourths of the several States, or by Conventions in three fourths thereof, as the one or the other Mode of Ratification may be proposed by the Congress; Provided that no Amendment which may be made prior to the Year One thousand eight hundred and eight shall in any Manner affect the first and fourth Clauses in the Ninth Section of the first Article; and that no State, without its Consent, shall be deprived of its equal Suffrage in the Senate.

ARTICLE VI.

[1] All Debts contracted and Engagements entered into, before the Adoption of this Constitution, shall be as valid against the United States under this Constitution, as under the Confederation.

[2] This Constitution, and the Laws of the United States which shall be made in Pursuance thereof; and all Treaties made, or which shall be made, under the Authority of the United States, shall be the supreme Law of the Land; and the Judges in every State shall be bound thereby, any Thing in the Constitution or Laws of any States to the Contrary notwithstanding.

[3] The Senators and Representatives before mentioned, and the Members of the several State Legislatures, and all executive and judicial Officers, both of the United States and of the several States, shall be bound by Oath or Affirmation, to support this Constitution; but no religious Test shall ever be required as a Qualification to any Office or public Trust under the United States.

ARTICLE VII.

The Ratification of the Conventions of nine States, shall be sufficient for the Establishment of this Constitution between the States so ratifying the Same.

DONE in Convention by the Unanimous Consent of the States present the Seventeenth Day of September in the Year of our Lord one thousand seven hundred and Eighty seven, and of the Independance of the United States of America the Twelfth **In Witness** whereof We have hereunto subscribed our Names,

G°: WASHINGTON —
Presidt. and Deputy from Virginia.

New Hampshire.

JOHN LANGDON   NICHOLAS GILMAN

Massachusetts.

NATHANIEL GORHAM   RUFUS KING

Connecticut.

WM. SAML. JOHNSON   ROGER SHERMAN

New York.

ALEXANDER HAMILTON

New Jersey.

WIL: LIVINGSTON   WM. PATERSON
DAVID BREARLEY   JONA: DAYTON

Pennsylvania.

B. FRANKLIN   THOS. FITZSIMONS
THOMAS MIFFLIN   JARED INGERSOLL
ROBT. MORRIS   JAMES WILSON
GEO. CLYMER   GOUV MORRIS

Delaware.

GEO: READ   RICHARD BASSETT
GUNNING BEDFORD JUN   JACO: BROOM
JOHN DICKINSON

Maryland.

JAMES MCHENRY   DANL. CARROLL
DAN OF ST THOS JENIFER

Virginia.

JOHN BLAIR —   JAMES MADISON JR.

North Carolina.

WM. BLOUNT   HU WILLIAMSON
RICHD. DOBBS SPAIGHT

South Carolina.

J. RUTLEDGE,   CHARLES PINCKNEY
CHARLES COTESWORTH   PIERCE BUTLER
   PINCKNEY

Georgia.

WILLIAM FEW   ABR BALDWIN

      Attest   WILLIAM JACKSON *Secretary*

BIBLIOGRAPHICAL NOTE

GOOD material on the period of the post-Revolutionary era is contained in *The Birth of the Republic, 1763–89* (1956) by Edmund S. Morgan and *The Creation of the American Republic, 1776–1787* (1969) by Gordon S. Wood. Also valuable are *The New Nation: A History of the United States During the Confederation, 1781–1789* (1950) by Merrill Jensen; *The American States During and After the American Revolution* (1924, reprinted 1969) by the Pulitzer Prize laureate, Allan Nevins; *E. Pluribus Unum: The Formation of the American Republic, 1776–1790* (1965) by Forrest McDonald and *The Confederation and the Constitution, 1783–1789* (1905) by Andrew C. McLaughlin.

Two fascinating state histories during this transition are Richard P. McCormick's *Experiment in Independence: New Jersey in the Critical Period, 1781–1789* (1950) and *The Practice and Politics of Fiat Finance: North Carolina in the Confederation, 1783–1789* (1955) by James R. Morrill.

A well-written account of our late 18th century statesmen is by the Pulitzer Prize historian, John Dos Passos, *The Men Who Made the Nation* (1957) while in *Seven Who Shaped Our Destiny: The Founding Fathers as Revolutionaries* (1973), Robert B. Morris has given us a fresh look at the charismatic leadership and staying power of Washington, John

Adams, Franklin, Jefferson, Hamilton, Madison and Jay.

Douglas Southall Freeman was awarded his second Pulitzer Prize in 1958 for the first six volumes of *George Washington* (1948 et seq.) and John A. Carroll and Mary W. Ashworth also shared in the Prize for completing the seventh and last volume after Freeman's death. James T. Flexner's four-volume series, *George Washington* (1965 et seq.) received a special Pulitzer award.

The multi-volume *Thomas Jefferson* (1948 et seq.) by Dumas Malone stands out as a major biographical accomplishment, while from Princeton comes valuable source material edited by Julian P. Boyd, *Papers of Thomas Jefferson* (1950 et seq.).

Another great leader has an able biographer in Page Smith, author of *John Adams* (2 volumes, 1962). The political philosophy of Adams is the focus of Edward Handler's *America and Europe in the Political Thought of John Adams* (1964) and *The Changing Political Thought of John Adams* (1966) by John R. Howe.

A basic fund of information on the genial statesman-philosopher, Benjamin Franklin, is Yale's series of 17 volumes, *The Papers of Benjamin Franklin,* published over the span from 1959 to 1972. For the life of this man of many accomplishments see Ralph Ketcham's *Benjamin Franklin* (1966) and *Benjamin Franklin: A Biography* (1938, reprinted 1956) by Carl van Doren.

Hamilton and Madison, two other major figures in the formative years of our Republic, are the subject of interesting studies. The former is treated by Broadus Mitchell in *Alexander Hamilton: Youth to Maturity, 1755–1788* (1957) and by John C. Miller in *Alexander Hamilton, Portrait in Paradox* (1959). Hamilton's leading role in the framing and adoption of the Constitution is well depicted in Clinton Rossiter's *Alexander Hamilton and the Constitution* (1964). Of the 6-volume series, *James Madison* (1941–1961) by Irving Brant, *The Nationalist, 1780–1787* and *The Father of The Constitution, 1787–1800* are especially illuminating.

Other important participants in our nation's early history are presented in Theodore Roosevelt's *Gouverneur Morris* (1888), W. G. Brown's *Life of Oliver Ellsworth* (1905) and Donald J. Smith's *John Jay: Founder of a State and a Nation* (1968). Page Smith's *James Wilson: Founding Father, 1742–1798* (1956) gives an account of this little-known but important statesman.

Max Farrand's *The Framing of the Constitution (1913)* remains the definitive account of the Federal Convention. Two other useful works are Charles Warren's *The Making of the Constitution* (1929, reprinted 1967) and Clinton Rossiter's *1787: The Grand Convention* (1966).

No account of the Convention is complete without *The Federalist,* written by Hamilton, Madison and Jay. While there are many editions of this classic, a good modern one is the Harvard version edited by Benjamin F. Wright (1961).

Opposition to adoption of the Constitution is chronicled in Jackson Turner Main's *The Antifederalists: Critics of the Constitution, 1781–1788* (1961) and

Robert A. Rutland's *The Ordeal of the Constitution: The Antifederalists and the Ratification Struggle of 1787–1788* (1966). The story of this struggle in one key state is told in Linda G. DePauw's *The Eleventh Pillar: New York State and the Federal Constitution* (1966).

The steps to provide added guarantees of our liberties is the central theme in Robert A. Rutland's *The Birth of the Bill of Rights, 1776–1791* (1955) and Irving Brant's *The Bill of Rights: Its Origins and Meaning* (1966).

Among the works dealing with the impact of economics upon the drafting of the Constitution are Charles A. Beard's *An Economic Interpretation of the Constitution of the United States* (1913; 17th printing, 1960) which gives some valuable and interesting facts about the formation of the Constitution and, a more modern book, *We The People: The Economic Origins of the Constitution* (1958) by Forrest McDonald.

Edward S. Corwin writes of American foreign policy during this period in *French Policy and the American Alliance* (1916) as does Paul A. Varg in *Foreign Policies of the Founding Fathers* (1968).

Useful books about early trade and industry include *The Roots of American Economic Growth, 1607–1861* (1965) by Stuart Bruchey; *The Emergence of a National Economy, 1775–1815* (1962) by Curtis P. Nettels; *Government and Labor in Early America* (1946, reprinted 1965) by Richard B. Morris and *The Maritime History of Massachusetts, 1783–1860* (1921) by Samuel Eliot Morison.

Francis S. Philbrick provides information on the

Northwest Territory in *The Rise of the West, 1754–1830* (1965) and this territory is the subject of a study, *The Old Northwest* (1918), by Frederic A. Ogg.

Especially recommended to those concerned with our cultural history during this period are *The Cultural Life of the New Nation, 1776–1830* (1960) by Russell B. Nye and *O Strange New World, American Culture: The Formative Years* (1964) by Howard Mumford Jones.

INDEX

A

Adams, John, on American Peace Commission, 9 *et seq.*; personal characteristics, 10; negotiates commercial treaty with the Netherlands, 11; on fisheries question, 13–14; on settlement of commercial indebtedness, 14–15; on granting compensation to Loyalists, 20; complains of trade restrictions for New England, 26

Adams, Samuel, and the Constitution, 151, 152

Albany Congress (1754), 49, 50

Annapolis Trade Convention (1786), 100–06

Anti-Federalist party, 147

Articles of Confederation, adoption (1777), 49–50; ratification (1781), 50, 57–59; based on Franklin's plan of union, 51–52; provisions, 52–54, 67–68, 86, 100; questions of land ownership delay ratification, 56–57, 58; financial power of Congress under, 86; failure of Commercial amendment of 1784, 99; relation to Constitution, 125, 131, 144; defects corrected in Constitution, 142; attempt at revision, 144–45; text, 175–189

Assenisipia, 69

B

Bancroft, George, *History of the Formation of the Constitution*, cited, 103 (note)

Biddle, Charles, *Autobiography*, on the Constitution, 141

Bowdoin, James, Governor of Massachusetts, and Shays' Rebellion, 94, 95

Bryce, Lord, cited, 13 (note)

C

Cambridge (Mass.), Shays' Rebellion at, 94

Canada, Loyalists go to, 19; Articles of Confederation on admitting, 67

Channing, Edward, *History of the United States*, cited, 21 (note), 61 (note)

Cherronesus, 69

China, trade with, 28

Combe, George, *Tour of the United States*, quoted, 45

Commerce, before Revolution, 24; conditions after Revolution, 24–27; commercial treaties, 26; development of trade with Far East, 28; phases of United States foreign trade, 28–29; domestic trade, 29–30; policy of reprisal, 97–99

Committees of Correspondence, 49